Table of Contents

Copyright © Houghton Mifflin Company. All rights reserved.

Organization and Format

In this booklet you will find assessments to be used at the end of each numbered unit in the HOUGHTON MIFFLIN ENGLISH pupil book as well as with the opening Getting Started: The Writing Process unit.

- **Getting Started: The Writing Process** An illustrated prompt, a list of descriptive details, and a graphic organizer are provided to help students plan and write a brief description.

- **Part 1: Grammar, Usage, and Mechanics Units** These unit tests assess the skills taught in all numbered lessons in the units in Part 1. Each Grammar unit test also includes a Proofreading section in which students correct usage and mechanics errors based on skills taught throughout the unit. In addition, each Grammar unit assessment concludes with a multiple-choice test that uses one of the Test Practice formats from the related pupil book unit. An End-of-Year Grammar Test appears as the last assessment in this booklet. This test will help you assess students' understanding of the most important grammar, usage, and mechanics skills taught in this level. You can give the entire assessment at one time or over several days. If your school has students keep portfolios that are passed on from teacher to teacher, the End-of-Year Grammar Test would be an excellent item to include.

- **Part 2: Writing Units** In the first section of each unit assessment in Part 2, students revise a passage by applying some of the focus skills taught in the related unit. The Proofreading section of each unit assessment directs students to find and correct errors by using skills addressed in the Grammar and Spelling Connections of the corresponding Writing unit and other important usage and mechanics skills taught previously. Finally, students plan and write a composition in response to a writing prompt that focuses on the unit writing mode.

The assessments utilize a variety of formats. Students respond by underlining, circling, marking, writing between lines, adding punctuation, using proofreading marks to correct mistakes, supplying words and phrases, and writing original paragraphs.

NOTE: For the proofreading paragraph in each Grammar unit assessment, proofreading marks should not be required; thus, the annotated pages show a simple cross-out-and-replace system.

Administering the Tests

For the Grammar unit assessments, students need only pencils and copies of the pages from the blackline masters.

For the Writing unit assessments, *students should have dictionaries easily available.* If possible, each student should have a dictionary at his or her desk. A Proofreading segment asks students to identify and correct misspelled words. If dictionaries are not available, you may ask students to circle words they think may be misspelled, and then grade this part of the test at your discretion.

Scoring and Recording

At the end of each assessment, you will find a scoring table to help you quickly determine percentage scores. These scores can be recorded on copies of the Individual Record Form printed on page 91 of this booklet. For monitoring progress of a group of students, scores can also be recorded on a copy of the Class Record Form printed on page 92 of this booklet.

Copyright © Houghton Mifflin Company. All rights reserved.

Name _____

Writing a Description

Write a Description 1–20. Look at the picture of the ice-cream cone. Write a description of it for someone your age. Describe how it looks, feels, and tastes.

Plan Before you write, plan your description. Label each detail in the following list with the word *looks, sounds, feels,* or *tastes* to show what sense or senses that detail describes. Then fill in the chart by writing each detail in the correct column.

dark brown cone _____

swirl of pale pink _____

crisp crunch against teeth _____

last bit of cone like damp cardboard _____

sharp tang of fresh strawberry _____

soothing, creamy softness _____

sugary sweetness _____

sprinkles dotted like bits of confetti _____

Ice-cream Cone			
Looks	**Sounds**	**Feels**	**Tastes**

Write your description on the next page.

Copyright © Houghton Mifflin Company. All rights reserved.

Grade 4: Getting Started: The Writing Process

Name _____

Writing a Description (continued from page 1)

Write Your Description Write a description of the ice-cream cone shown in the picture on page 1. Beginning and ending sentences are given below. Use the details in your chart to write supporting sentences that describe the ice-cream cone. Use exact words, and elaborate your sentences to make your description clear and vivid.

I will never get tired of strawberry ice-cream cones. _____

_____

_____

_____

_____

_____

_____

_____

_____

_____

_____

_____

_____

_____

_____

_____

_____

After I lick my lips, I start dreaming of the next time I'll place the same order.

Number correct 10 11 12 13 14 15 16 17 18 19 20
Percent correct 50 55 60 65 70 75 80 85 90 95 100

Copyright © Houghton Mifflin Company. All rights reserved.

Grade 4: Getting Started: The Writing Process

Name _____

The Sentence

What Is a Sentence? Underline each group of words that is a sentence.

1. We took our bikes to the park.

2. Locked them carefully.

3. The old, broken swings.

4. Joe went down the slide.

Statements and Questions; Commands and Exclamations Write each sentence correctly.

5. please open the window _____

6. will you help me _____

7. what a mess they made _____

8. we should clean it up _____

9. where shall we start _____

10. pick up those toys _____

Subjects and Predicates Draw a line between each complete subject and complete predicate.

11. Pandas are not really bears.

12. My family saw two pandas at the National Zoo.

13. Both furry animals played.

Simple Subjects The complete subject of each sentence is underlined. Circle each simple subject.

14. <u>My older sister</u> uses Dad's home computer.

15. <u>Sharon</u> solves problems with it.

16. <u>Some friends of mine</u> have their own computers.

17. <u>The keyboard of the computer</u> is easily broken.

Copyright © Houghton Mifflin Company. All rights reserved.

Name _____

The Sentence (continued from page 3)

Simple Predicates The complete predicate of each sentence is underlined. Circle each simple predicate.

18. I spilled apple juice on the keyboard last week.

19. Dad hollered.

20. He has another computer at his office, though.

21. Sharon's friend uses the computer often.

22. She and I play computer games.

Correcting Run-on Sentences Rewrite each run-on sentence correctly.

23. The air was cold we built a fire.

_____

24. Our tent leaked, we patched the holes.

_____

Proofreading 25–32. Proofread the paragraphs below. Correct the five mistakes in punctuation and three mistakes in capital letters.

Example: I just saw my first tuatara. ~~w~~**W**hat an interesting animal it is!

The tuatara is the oldest, coldest, and slowest of all reptiles? It has lived on Earth for nearly two hundred million years. This animal is found on a few tiny islands in New Zealand. it lives in the nests of sea birds. The male can be over two feet long, but the female is shorter both can live as long as seventy years.

Temperatures as low as 45°F are quite comfortable for this reptile. It breathes only about once an hour one or two earthworms a week satisfy its hunger.

The tuatara has three eyes The third eye cannot see objects, but it can tell light from dark. What a strange animal this is.

Copyright © Houghton Mifflin Company. All rights reserved.

Name _____

The Sentence *(continued from page 4)*

The Sentence 33–40. Read each passage below and find the numbered, underlined parts. Choose the answer that shows the best way to capitalize and punctuate each underlined part. Fill in the circle next to that answer.

Which bus did you take? On the
(33)
field trip? We were on Bus 4. What a

disaster that was the air-conditioning
(34)
broke down? a girl got sick and a boy
(35)
got a bloody nose. Then the bus got a
(36)
flat tire.

Have you ever been to the

seashore? have you ever seen an animal
(37)
walking sideways across the sand. This
(38)
creature is called a crab a crab is an
(39)
animal with a jointed shell and ten

legs The front legs end in big claws.
(40)

33. Ⓐ take? on
   Ⓑ take. On
   Ⓒ take on
   Ⓓ Correct as it is

34. Ⓕ was! The
   Ⓖ was? the
   Ⓗ was! the
   Ⓙ Correct as it is

35. Ⓐ down a
   Ⓑ down. a
   Ⓒ down. A
   Ⓓ Correct as it is

36. Ⓕ nose? Then
   Ⓖ nose. then
   Ⓗ nose then
   Ⓙ Correct as it is

37. Ⓐ seashore. Have
   Ⓑ seashore! Have
   Ⓒ seashore? Have
   Ⓓ Correct as it is

38. Ⓕ sand. this
   Ⓖ sand this
   Ⓗ sand? This
   Ⓙ Correct as it is

39. Ⓐ crab! a
   Ⓑ crab. A
   Ⓒ crab? a
   Ⓓ Correct as it is

40. Ⓕ legs. The
   Ⓖ legs. the
   Ⓗ legs? The
   Ⓙ Correct as it is

Number correct	20	21	22	23	24	25	26	27	28	29	30	31	32	33	34	35	36	37	38	39	40
Percent correct	50	53	55	58	60	63	65	68	70	73	75	78	80	83	85	88	90	93	95	98	100

Grade 4: Unit 1   The Sentence

Copyright © Houghton Mifflin Company. All rights reserved.

Name _____

Nouns

What Is a Noun? Underline the nouns in each sentence.

1. The store had a big sale.

2. Stan has saved his money.

3. The price of skates is low now.

4. The ice on the pond has melted.

Common and Proper Nouns Write the common and the proper nouns from each sentence. Use capital letters correctly in the proper nouns.

5. The twins live in new mexico. _____

6. Uncle hank is coming for thanksgiving. _____

7. Is dania sanchez interested in the planets? _____

8. My sister is a teacher in miami, florida. _____

Singular and Plural Nouns Underline the correct noun in ( ). If it is singular, write *S*. If it is plural, write *P*.

9. This (pet, pets) needs a lot of care. _____

10. Liat cleaned both (cage, cages). _____

11. Her hamsters play in several (box, boxes). _____

12. Bill feeds his dog two (sandwich, sandwiches) for lunch. _____

13. Yesterday he took the dog on a (bus, buses). _____

Nouns Ending with *y* Complete each sentence with the plural form of the noun in ( ).

14. This hotel has two _____. (lobby)

15. The desk clerk found the _____ to our rooms. (key)

16. Three _____ were buzzing outside the window. (fly)

17. Room service brought a dish of _____. (strawberry)

Copyright © Houghton Mifflin Company. All rights reserved.

Nouns *(continued from page 7)*

More Plural Nouns Complete each sentence with the plural form of the noun in ( ).

18. A pair of _____ pulled the heavy wagon. (ox)

19. The _____ helped with the animals. (child)

20. Our cat chased two _____ in the barn. (mouse)

21. The dog rounded up the _____. (sheep)

Singular Possessive Nouns Write each group of words another way. Use the possessive form of each underlined noun.

22. dish that the <u>dog</u> uses _____

23. spaceship of <u>Rexdar</u> _____

24. car belonging to the <u>woman</u> _____

25. name of the <u>baby</u> _____

Plural Possessive Nouns Complete each group of words with the possessive form of the noun in ( ).

26. the _____ cages (monkeys)

27. the _____ supplies (armies)

28. the _____ wool (sheep)

29. the _____ lungs (lizards)

Copyright © Houghton Mifflin Company. All rights reserved.

Nouns *(continued from page 8)*

Proofreading 30–37. Proofread the paragraphs below. Find one incorrect proper noun, four incorrect plural nouns, and three incorrect possessive nouns. Correct the mistakes.

Example: The ~~mayors~~' office is in the town hall.
          mayor's

> Vickys' father is the mayor of our town. Mr. Wade always
>
> performs his dutys with a cheerful smile. The childs in our
>
> school look forward to his visits. He often gives us little toyes.
>
> He makes funny speechs too.
>
>   Mr. Wade also sells mens' shoes in his store near Glen park.
>
> In the window of his store, a large photograph shows Mr.
>
> Wade's sons dressed up as turkeys for Thanksgiving. The boy's
>
> feathers are orange and black.

➜

Copyright © Houghton Mifflin Company. All rights reserved.

Nouns *(continued from page 9)*

Nouns 38–45. Choose the best way to write the underlined part of each sentence. Fill in the circle beside that answer. If there is no mistake, fill in the circle beside the last answer.

38. Elena's birthday is on <u>Flag Day</u>.
   Ⓐ flag day
   Ⓑ Flag day
   Ⓒ flag Day
   Ⓓ (No mistakes)

39. Our new <u>Dog is named bo</u>.
   Ⓕ dog is named Bo
   Ⓖ dog is named bo
   Ⓗ Dog is named Bo
   Ⓙ (No mistakes)

40. Movers packed fifty <u>boxs</u>.
   Ⓐ boxies
   Ⓑ box
   Ⓒ boxes
   Ⓓ (No mistakes)

41. The television show was about a family of <u>monkey</u>.
   Ⓕ monkees
   Ⓖ monkeys
   Ⓗ monkies
   Ⓙ (No mistakes)

42. Two <u>woman</u> demonstrated karate for the students.
   Ⓐ women
   Ⓑ womans
   Ⓒ womens
   Ⓓ (No mistakes)

43. Several <u>factories</u> were closed down.
   Ⓕ factory
   Ⓖ factorys
   Ⓗ factory's
   Ⓙ (No mistakes)

44. <u>Susans'</u> toothpaste tastes like cinnamon.
   Ⓐ Susans
   Ⓑ Susan's
   Ⓒ Susan'
   Ⓓ (No mistakes)

45. All of the <u>mens</u> jackets are on sale.
   Ⓕ mens'
   Ⓖ menses'
   Ⓗ men's
   Ⓙ (No mistakes)

Copyright © Houghton Mifflin Company. All rights reserved.

Number correct	22	23	24	25	26	27	28	29	30	31	32	33	34	35	36	37	38	39	40	41
Percent correct	49	51	53	56	58	60	62	64	67	69	71	73	76	78	80	82	84	87	89	91

Number correct	42	43	44	45
Percent correct	93	96	98	100

Grade 4: Unit 2   Nouns

Name _____

Verbs

Action Verbs Underline the action verb in each sentence.

1. Fred prepared a pie.

2. First, he mixed the crust.

3. Sue helped him.

4. Sue peeled a dozen apples.

5. The oven made a funny noise.

6. The pie baked for forty minutes.

Main Verbs and Helping Verbs Underline the helping verb in each sentence. Circle the main verb.

7. We had waited for you at the fairgrounds.

8. Yolanda is showing her prize pig.

9. The dog has slept under a tree.

10. The band will play three songs.

11. I am leaving for home now.

Present, Past, and Future Underline the verb in each sentence. Then write *present, past,* or *future.*

12. We chatted about the weather. _____

13. Yesterday it rained all morning. _____

14. Snow will fall Friday. _____

15. Usually the wind blows from the south. _____

16. The sun will shine this weekend. _____

Subject-Verb Agreement Underline the correct verb form in ( ).

17. Pigs (eat, eats) turnips.

18. The farmer (plant, plants) turnips in July.

19. In November he (harvest, harvests) them.

20. Mom and Dad (enjoy, enjoys) mashed turnips.

Copyright © Houghton Mifflin Company. All rights reserved.

Name _____

Verbs *(continued from page 11)*

Spelling the Present Tense Write the present tense of the verb in ( ).

21. Our leaky radiator _____ us. (worry)

22. A bucket _____ the water. (catch)

23. The bucket _____ often. (overflow)

24. Our neighbor, Rusty, _____ the leak from time to time. (fix)

Spelling the Past Tense Write the past tense of the verb in ( ).

25. Mr. Drummond _____ Doug and Marcy. (employ)

26. Together, they _____ Mr. Drummond's papers. (copy)

27. Doug _____ his job. (like)

28. He _____ in the elevator. (hum)

The Past with Helping Verbs Write *have* or *has* to complete each sentence correctly.

29. The students _____ practiced the song.

30. Lamont _____ played it on his guitar.

31. Our teacher _____ planned a concert.

32. We _____ helped her.

Irregular Verbs Write the correct past form of the verb in ( ).

33. Rocky and Louie have _____ a garden. (begin)

34. Last year they _____ tomatoes. (grow)

35. The year before they had _____ corn and beans. (grow)

36. Louie almost _____ the shovel. (break)

Copyright © Houghton Mifflin Company. All rights reserved.

Name _____

Verbs *(continued from page 12)*

The Special Verb *be* Underline the correct form of the verb *be* in ( ).

37. The girls (is, are) sisters.

38. Last year I (was, were) in their math class.

39. They (was, were) good students.

40. Math (is, are) still their favorite subject.

Contractions with *not* Write a contraction to replace the underlined word or words.

41. Wild gorillas <u>do not</u> live in North America. _____

42. Gorillas <u>are not</u> strong swimmers. _____

43. Apes <u>cannot</u> eat unripe fruit. _____

44. Adult female gorillas <u>will not</u> groom each other. _____

45. Hunters <u>should not</u> kill gorillas for their skins. _____

Proofreading 46–52. Proofread the paragraphs below. Find one incorrect contraction and six incorrect verb forms. Correct the mistakes.

Example: I ~~has~~ ^{have} enjoyed my pet indri, a kind of mammal related to the monkey.

> My indri's name is Brat, and he looks like a little white monkey. He comes
>
> from an island in the Indian Ocean. Sometimes Brat clutchs my hand, and
>
> sometimes he walks alone. He steadys himself with his long, slender arms. Still,
>
> he have tripped once or twice.
>
> Yesterday morning at six o'clock, Brat hoped up onto my bed. He was
>
> hungry. I was still very sleepy, but Brat would'nt leave me alone! I gave him
>
> some tender leaves for his breakfast. All too soon, Brat had ate enough, and he
>
> wanted his bath. I grumbled a little, but then I washed him in the sink. Next, I
>
> dryed him with a face cloth. Brat was clean, fluffy, and ready for more fun!

Copyright © Houghton Mifflin Company. All rights reserved.

Name _____

Verbs *(continued from page 13)*

Verbs 53–60. Read each passage. Choose the line that shows the mistake. Fill in the circle beside that answer. If there is no mistake, fill in the circle beside the last answer.

53. Ⓐ Max has growed.
    Ⓑ He can't fit into his jacket anymore.
    Ⓒ Yesterday he wore a sweater.
    Ⓓ (No mistakes)

54. Ⓕ Last year Cristina collects
    Ⓖ shells. Now she collects fans.
    Ⓗ Luckily she has a big room!
    Ⓙ (No mistakes)

55. Ⓐ An owl lives near our house.
    Ⓑ It screechs so loudly at night!
    Ⓒ Last night it drove me crazy.
    Ⓓ (No mistakes)

56. Ⓕ My baby cousins is cute. Philip
    Ⓖ sits and watches everybody.
    Ⓗ Henri doesn't sit still at all.
    Ⓙ (No mistakes)

57. Ⓐ Tomorrow, Walker will give
    Ⓑ a piano recital. He plays well.
    Ⓒ He have studied for many years.
    Ⓓ (No mistakes)

58. Ⓕ Dad took me to the bowling
    Ⓖ alley on Monday. I threw the ball
    Ⓗ so badly. I dont ever improve!
    Ⓙ (No mistake)

59. Ⓐ The storm began at noon.
    Ⓑ After the rain stoped, we went
    Ⓒ outside. We took a long walk.
    Ⓓ (No mistakes)

60. Ⓕ I am baking a carrot cake.
    Ⓖ The oven timer buzzes loudly.
    Ⓗ The cake is'nt done yet.
    Ⓙ (No mistakes)

Number correct	30	31	32	33	34	35	36	37	38	39	40	41	42	43	44	45	46	47	48	49
Percent correct	50	52	53	55	57	58	60	62	63	65	67	68	70	72	73	75	77	78	80	82

Number correct	50	51	52	53	54	55	56	57	58	59	60
Percent correct	83	85	87	89	90	92	93	95	97	98	100

Copyright © Houghton Mifflin Company. All rights reserved.

Name _____

Adjectives

What Is an Adjective? Underline each adjective. Circle the noun it describes. Do not underline *a* and *the*.

1. The frisky, new puppy tumbled in the grass.

2. It saw two busy bees in the garden.

3. The playful puppy chased after the bees.

4. Soon the puppy had a sore nose from a nasty sting.

Adjectives After *be* Underline each adjective that comes after a form of the verb *be*. Circle the word it describes.

5. Some movies are exciting.

6. That film was dull though.

7. Even the popcorn was stale!

8. My neck is stiff.

9. Sometimes I am cranky.

10. Julie was noisy during the movie.

Using *a*, *an*, and *the* Underline the correct article in ( ).

11. We found (a, an) strange thing in (an, the) garage.

12. It was (a, an) oil painting of (a, an) wooded scene.

13. (A, The) painting was dusty but not torn.

14. (A, An) old painting can be (a, an) valuable find!

Making Comparisons Write the correct form of the adjective in ( ).

15. In Iowa, July is the _____ month of the year. (hot)

16. This is the _____ day ever. (warm)

17. Yesterday was _____ than today. (sunny)

18. This thunderstorm is _____ than the one last week. (close)

Copyright © Houghton Mifflin Company. All rights reserved.

Name _____

Adjectives *(continued from page 15)*

Comparing with *more* and *most* Write the correct form of the adjective in ( ).

19. This event is _____ than Columbus Day. (exciting)

20. Pearl has the _____ costume of all. (unusual)

21. She is dressed as the _____ princess in Idaho. (mysterious)

22. Her hat is even _____ than her outfit. (fantastic)

Comparing with *good* and *bad* Write the correct form of the word in ( ).

23. The _____ painting of the two will take the prize. (good)

24. My painting style is _____ than Kaye's. (bad)

25. The _____ part of the whole contest is the judging. (bad)

26. Winning is the _____ feeling of all. (good)

➡

Copyright © Houghton Mifflin Company. All rights reserved.

Grade 4: Unit 4   Adjectives

Name _____

Adjectives *(continued from page 16)*

Proofreading 27–34. Proofread the paragraphs below. Find seven mistakes in comparing with adjectives. Find one mistake in using *a* or *an*. Correct the mistakes.

more nervous

Example: The octopus is ~~nervouser~~ than its relative, the squid.

The octopus and the squid are both mollusks. The octopus

is the most interesting animal of the two. Its brain is larger

than the squid's. In fact, the octopus is one of the intelligentest

animals in the world. Only mammals are more smart.

A octopus lives a shy, quiet life. It swims here and there to

find food, but it is happyest at home in its cave at the bottom

of the sea. Crabs are its favorite food.

Of the many kinds of octopus, the bigest measures almost

thirty-two feet across. It lives in the North Pacific Ocean. The

most smallest kind is only two inches wide. It lives in the

Indian Ocean.

The octopus will not usually bite a human being. The

worse octopus bite ever happened off the coast of Australia

in 1967.

→

Copyright © Houghton Mifflin Company. All rights reserved.

Grade 4: Unit 4 Adjectives

Name _____

Adjectives *(continued from page 17)*

Adjectives 35–40. Look at each underlined part of the paragraph. Find the correct way to write the underlined part in each numbered line. Fill in the circle beside that answer. If the part is already correct, fill in the circle beside the last answer, "Correct as it is."

(35)   One of the <u>scaryest</u> things in the world is

(36)   an earthquake. Even the <u>smallest</u> quake feels odd.

(37)   A <u>biger</u> one is terrifying! One of the world's

(38)   <u>worse</u> quakes struck Los Angeles in 1994.

(39)   An even <u>badder</u> quake rocked Japan in 1923.

(40)   The <u>terriblest</u> earthquakes can destroy whole towns.

35. Ⓐ scarier
    Ⓑ most scaryest
    Ⓒ scariest
    Ⓓ Correct as it is

36. Ⓕ smalest
    Ⓖ smaller
    Ⓗ most small
    Ⓙ Correct as it is

37. Ⓐ bigger
    Ⓑ more bigger
    Ⓒ more big
    Ⓓ Correct as it is

38. Ⓕ most worse
    Ⓖ worser
    Ⓗ worst
    Ⓙ Correct as it is

39. Ⓐ more bad
    Ⓑ baddest
    Ⓒ worse
    Ⓓ Correct as it is

40. Ⓕ most terrible
    Ⓖ more terribler
    Ⓗ most terriblest
    Ⓙ Correct as it is

Copyright © Houghton Mifflin Company. All rights reserved.

Number correct	20	21	22	23	24	25	26	27	28	29	30	31	32	33	34	35	36	37	38	39	40
Percent correct	50	53	55	58	60	63	65	68	70	73	75	78	80	83	85	88	90	93	95	98	100

Grade 4: Unit 4   Adjectives

Name _____

Capitalization and Punctuation

Correct Sentences Correct these sentences and run-ons. Cross out letters and add capital letters where they are needed. Add end marks.

1. come to our tea party

2. didn't you receive an invitation

3. my mother is wearing her violet blouse do you like it

4. how beautiful the table looks

5. don't touch the flowers they are very delicate

Names of People and Pets Correct these sentences. Cross out letters and add capital letters where they are needed.

6. First, jane franklin arrived with her father.

7. Her cat, zizi, came along too.

8. The guest of honor, dr. w. d. may, arrived next.

9. Soon aunt doris introduced everyone.

10. At noon, mother announced lunch.

Names of Places and Things Correct these sentences. Cross out letters and add capital letters where they are needed.

11. French people celebrate bastille day on july 14.

12. The best month for a visit to paris is september.

13. A popular sight in the city is the eiffel tower.

14. The newburg french club returned from a trip last monday.

15. Members visited mont blanc, a mountain in france.

Copyright © Houghton Mifflin Company. All rights reserved.

Name _____

Capitalization and Punctuation *(continued from page 19)*

Abbreviations Write the abbreviations for the underlined words.

16. <u>Doctor</u> Kim Chan _____

17. 1462 Fair Oaks <u>Road</u>, Cleveland, <u>Ohio</u> _____

18. <u>Post Office Box</u> 56 _____

19. <u>Mister</u> William Bailey <u>Junior</u> _____

20. <u>Friday</u>, <u>August</u> 8 _____

Commas in a Series Add commas where they are needed.

21. Oscar Ann and Lamar put on a play.

22. Lamar wrote practiced and acted.

23. Oscar got scenery costumes and a curtain.

24. The play was funny interesting and enjoyable.

More Uses for Commas Add commas where they are needed.

25. Do you feel better Isabel than you did yesterday?

26. Yes I'm going back to school tomorrow.

27. Well I'll look forward to seeing you.

28. Hannah do you understand our homework assignment?

29. Yes let me explain it to you.

Quotation Marks Add quotation marks to each sentence that needs them. Underline any sentence that does not need quotation marks.

30. Look out for the car! shouted Pilar.

31. Thanks! exclaimed Vera as she jumped out of the way.

32. Pilar asked, Didn't you see it?

33. Vera answered that she was daydreaming.

34. Will you be more careful now? asked Pilar.

35. Vera promised that she would.

Copyright © Houghton Mifflin Company. All rights reserved.

Name _____

Capitalization and Punctuation *(continued from page 20)*

Quotations Correct each quotation. Add punctuation marks and capital letters where they are needed.

36. Where are my fiddlers three asked Old King Cole

37. Little Miss Muffet exclaimed these curds taste awful

38. That candlestick is too tall said Jack

39. The owl warned the pussycat don't fall overboard

Titles Write each title correctly.

40. highlights _____

41. child of fire _____

42. the downtown news _____

43. number the stars _____

Proofreading 44–49. Proofread the paragraph below. Find two mistakes in capital letters and four missing or incorrect punctuation marks. Correct the mistakes.

Example: The play is in a book called Plays <u>F̶or Special Days</u>.

> Ms. Bradley said that we will put on a play to celebrate
>
> Martin Luther King day. She asked, "Who wants to try out for
>
> the main parts? Well almost all of us raised our hands. I tried
>
> out for dr. King. So did Jason, Matt and Carlos. What a shock
>
> it was when I actually got the part. I'm nervous about
>
> forgetting my lines, but Mom said that she'll help me
>
> rehearse.

Copyright © Houghton Mifflin Company. All rights reserved.

Capitalization and Punctuation (continued from page 21)

Capitalization and Punctuation 50–55. Read the passage and look at the numbered, underlined parts. Choose the answer that shows the best way to write each underlined part. Fill in the circle beside that answer.

The author Charles Dickens was born in <u>england on February</u> 7, 1812.
(50)

Unfortunately, his father often had serious money troubles. Charles had to leave

school and go to <u>work soon</u> he got a job with a <u>Newspaper in london</u>. In 1836,
(51)　　　　　　　　　　　　　　　　　(52)

Dickens married <u>miss catherine hogarth</u>. That same year, he wrote and published
(53)

<u>the pickwick papers</u>, his first book. <u>It was brilliant. it was funny.</u> It was popular.
(54)　　　　　　　　　　　　　　　　(55)

50. Ⓐ England on february
　　Ⓑ England on February
　　Ⓒ england on february
　　Ⓓ Correct as it is

51. Ⓕ work. soon
　　Ⓖ work. Soon
　　Ⓗ work? Soon
　　Ⓙ Correct as it is

52. Ⓐ Newspaper in London
　　Ⓑ newspaper in london
　　Ⓒ newspaper in London
　　Ⓓ Correct as it is

53. Ⓕ miss Catherine Hogarth
　　Ⓖ Miss Catherine Hogarth
　　Ⓗ Miss catherine hogarth
　　Ⓙ Correct as it is

54. Ⓐ The pickwick papers
　　Ⓑ The Pickwick Papers
　　Ⓒ The Pickwick Papers
　　Ⓓ Correct as it is

55. Ⓕ It was brilliant it was funny and
　　　it was popular.
　　Ⓖ It was brilliant funny and
　　　popular.
　　Ⓗ It was brilliant, funny, and
　　　popular.
　　Ⓙ Correct as it is

Number correct	28	29	30	31	32	33	34	35	36	37	38	39	40	41	42	43	44	45
Percent correct	51	53	55	56	58	60	62	64	65	67	69	71	73	75	76	78	80	82

Number correct	46	47	48	49	50	51	52	53	54	55
Percent correct	84	85	87	89	91	93	95	96	98	100

Copyright © Houghton Mifflin Company. All rights reserved.

Name _____

Pronouns

What Is a Pronoun? Circle the pronoun that takes the place of the underlined word or words.

1. "Hal and I hiked up into the canyon," <u>Kit</u> said.

2. The sun warmed <u>Hal and Kit</u>, and they slowed down.

3. "Soon the sun was beating down on us," <u>the boys</u> explained.

Subject Pronouns Write the subject pronoun that could take the place of the underlined word or words.

4. <u>Bev and I</u> take long rides on our bikes. _____

5. <u>The bikes</u> stay in good repair. _____

6. Sometimes <u>Dad</u> joins us for a trip. _____

Object Pronouns Write the object pronoun that could take the place of the underlined words.

7. I took a picture of <u>Nate and Eileen</u>. _____

8. Nate bought a dinosaur book for <u>his sister</u>. _____

9. Eileen liked <u>the book</u> very much. _____

Using *I* and *me* Underline the correct word or words in ( ).

10. Langston, Pepe, and (I, me) planned a party for Al.

11. Pepe asked Langston and (I, me) for help with the decorations.

12. (He and I, I and he) found some blue balloons.

Possessive Pronouns Write the possessive pronoun that could take the place of the underlined word or words.

13. <u>Meg's</u> prism is made of glass. I saw _____ prism yesterday.

14. <u>The sun's</u> rays shine on us. _____ rays keep us warm.

15. <u>The twins'</u> cameras are new. _____ cameras use a new kind of film.

Copyright © Houghton Mifflin Company. All rights reserved.

Name _____

Pronouns *(continued from page 23)*

Contractions with Pronouns Write a contraction to replace the underlined words in each sentence.

16. <u>I am</u> fond of my pet, Ducky. _____

17. <u>She is</u> a mammal with a broad, flat, hairless snout. _____

18. She laid two eggs, and <u>they will</u> hatch in ten days. _____

19. <u>We are</u> giving her young to Mr. Marcos at the zoo. _____

Pronouns and Homophones Underline the correct word in ( ).

20. Is that (your, you're) puppy?

21. (Your, You're) giving it too much dog food.

22. (Its, It's) such a pretty puppy.

23. (There, Their, They're) are pretty ones next door too.

24. (There, Their, They're) eyes are especially beautiful.

25. (There, Their, They're) very noisy, though.

Proofreading 26–30. Proofread these paragraphs. Find four incorrect pronouns. Find one pronoun that is in the wrong position in the sentence. Correct the mistakes.

Example: ~~I and Bernice~~ ^{**Bernice and I**} visited Philadelphia and had a great time ^{**there**} ~~their~~.

> Bernice and I took an exciting trip on a train. Our old neighbor, Mrs. Lincoln,
>
> met her and I at the train station. I had not seen Mrs. Lincoln for almost two years.
>
> Mrs. Lincoln gave me a big hug. She said, "Your so tall now, Connie, and
>
> what long hair you have! How do you do those braids? Their great!"
>
> Mrs. Lincoln drove us to her home near the river and served us some
>
> delicious cold chicken sandwiches. That night us slept in a big brass bed
>
> with fat white pillows and soft, fluffy blankets. Mrs. Lincoln sang a lullaby to
>
> me and Bernice from the porch below our window.

Copyright © Houghton Mifflin Company. All rights reserved.

Pronouns *(continued from page 24)*

Pronouns 31–35. Read the passage all the way through once. Then look at the underlined parts. Decide if they need to be changed or if they are fine as they are. Choose the best answer from the choices given. Fill in the circle beside that answer.

Last week, <u>me and my sister</u>
(31)
were jumping rope outside. Two of

our neighbors were arguing.

"<u>You're</u> tree is dropping leaves
(32)
onto my driveway," said Mr.

Nodden to Mr. Benoit. <u>He</u> stared
(33)
angrily at him.

The argument seemed silly to

<u>my sister and I. We</u> began to giggle,
(34)
and the men's faces turned red.

They stopped <u>their</u> quarrel and
(35)
made peace.

31. Ⓐ my sister and me
    Ⓑ I and my sister
    Ⓒ my sister and I
    Ⓓ (No change)

32. Ⓕ Your
    Ⓖ You
    Ⓗ Your'
    Ⓙ (No change)

33. Ⓐ The man
    Ⓑ Mr. Benoit
    Ⓒ His neighbor
    Ⓓ (No change)

34. Ⓕ my sister and me. We
    Ⓖ my sister and I. Us
    Ⓗ I and my sister. We
    Ⓙ (No change)

35. Ⓐ They're
    Ⓑ There
    Ⓒ They
    Ⓓ (No change)

Copyright © Houghton Mifflin Company. All rights reserved.

Number correct	18	19	20	21	22	23	24	25	26	27	28	29	30	31	32	33	34	35
Percent correct	51	54	57	60	63	66	69	72	75	78	81	84	85	89	91	94	97	100

Grade 4: Unit 6   Pronouns

Name _____

Adverbs and Prepositions

What Is an Adverb? Underline each adverb. Circle the verb it describes.

1. Finally, my sister and I left the house.

2. Koko and I ran fast.

3. I opened the big library door, and we went inside.

4. The science movie soon began.

5. Everyone sat quietly.

Comparing with Adverbs Write the correct form of the adverb in ( ).

6. Gwen arrives _____ than Pedro. (late)

7. Her train runs _____ than his. (slowly)

8. Of all the kids, he lives _____ to the school. (near)

9. Of all the class, Gwen talks _____. (cheerfully)

10. She eats her snack _____ than Pedro. (fast)

Using *good* and *well* Write *good* or *well* to complete each sentence correctly.

11. Steve makes _____ waffles.

12. He cooks _____.

13. He is also _____ at sports.

14. Steve does many things _____.

Negatives Underline the correct word to complete each sentence.

15. We don't have (no, any) milk for breakfast.

16. Dad didn't buy (any, none) yesterday.

17. Won't (anybody, nobody) go to the store?

18. The stores (are, aren't) never open this early.

Copyright © Houghton Mifflin Company. All rights reserved.

Adverbs and Prepositions (continued from page 27)

What Is a Preposition? For each sentence, underline the prepositional phrase once and the preposition twice.

19. The birds flew across the sky.

20. A crow landed on the pine.

21. The robin has straw in its beak.

22. The parrot talked during the TV show.

23. Birdseed was scattered over the snow.

Proofreading 24–27. Proofread the paragraph below. Find two mistakes in comparing with adverbs, one mistake in using *good* or *well,* and one mistake in using negatives. Correct the mistakes.

Example: None of our birds lay ~~most~~ *more* frequently than my hen Annabel.

Annabel lays an egg almost every day. She has two chicks,

Maynard and Bit. Bit comes to my call quicklier than

Maynard. Of all the chicks we've ever had, Maynard cheeps

louder. I can hear him well when I bring the food. Annabel

usually keeps him quiet, though. Both chicks mind Annabel

good. They don't have no real feathers yet. Soft yellow down

still covers them.

➡

Copyright © Houghton Mifflin Company. All rights reserved.

Name _____

Adverbs and Prepositions (continued from page 28)

Adverbs 28–35. Read each paragraph below. Choose the line that shows the mistake. Fill in the circle beside that answer. If there is no mistake, fill in the circle beside the last answer.

28. (A) On Field Day, two teams
    (B) played tug of war. The red
    (C) team pulled hardest.
    (D) (No mistakes)

29. (F) Martina cooks good.
    (G) She helps her father make
    (H) dinner on weekends.
    (J) (No mistakes)

30. (A) I never got none of the
    (B) strawberries. Someone
    (C) else ate them all.
    (D) (No mistakes)

31. (F) Otto felt shy at the party.
    (G) He didn't know nobody.
    (H) He wanted to leave.
    (J) (No mistakes)

32. (A) Kaia danced in the show.
    (B) Of all the dancers, she
    (C) leaped higher.
    (D) (No mistakes)

33. (F) Joe and Sam mopped the
    (G) floor. Sam worked more
    (H) carefullier than Joe did.
    (J) (No mistakes)

34. (A) I took three trains. The last
    (B) one traveled most fastest
    (C) and most smoothly.
    (D) (No mistakes)

35. (F) Jasmine's mother paints
    (G) well. She hasn't ever
    (H) taken an art lesson.
    (J) (No mistakes)

Copyright © Houghton Mifflin Company. All rights reserved.

Number correct	18	19	20	21	22	23	24	25	26	27	28	29	30	31	32	33	34	35
Percent correct	51	54	57	60	63	66	69	72	75	78	81	84	85	89	91	94	97	100

Grade 4: Unit 7   Adverbs and Prepositions

Name _____

Writing a Personal Narrative

Revising 1–4. Revise the following personal narrative, using the directions in the box. Use the space above each line, on the sides, and below the narrative for your changes.

- Take out one unimportant sentence.
- Add at least one detail to a sentence, telling how the umbrella looked.
- Change one sentence into dialogue.
- Write an ending that tells how the story worked out.

The Useful Umbrella

The ugliest present I ever received was an umbrella with a

map of the world on it. I stuck it in the back of a closet and

never used it. It rains a lot in Seattle, where I live.

One night I had to draw a map of Spain. I had left my

social studies book at school, and I couldn't find a map at

home. My sister reminded me about the umbrella.

When I found the umbrella, I was so relieved. I opened the

dusty folds, and there was Spain, clearly outlined and labeled!

Copyright © Houghton Mifflin Company. All rights reserved.

Name _____

Writing a Personal Narrative *(continued from page 31)*

Proofreading 5–10. Proofread this personal narrative to fix the six mistakes. Use proofreading marks to make your corrections.

- Find two mistakes in verb tense.
- Find one missing end mark.
- Find a group of words that is not a sentence. Fix it by adding it to a complete sentence.
- Find two misspelled words with a short vowel sound before a consonant.

Proofreading Marks

¶ Indent
∧ Add
⌒ Delete
≡ Capital letter
／ Small letter

The Dentist Drill Blues

Last week I visit the dentist for a checkup. I had a nasty

surprise. Dr. Love said I needed a filling!

When I went back to the dentist the neaxt week, I was really

scared. I was sure the experience would be painful Dr. Love

put on some nice music. She told me to relax and breathe

deeply. Then she drill my tooth. She filled the hole. I hardly

feelt any pain. Finally, she told me I could leave.

On my way out. Dr. Love gave me a new toothbrush. She

said I had been brave. "It was nothing," I said, and I meant it!

Copyright © Houghton Mifflin Company. All rights reserved.

Name _____

Writing a Personal Narrative (continued from page 32)

Writing Prompt: A Personal Narrative 11–30. Follow the prompt below to plan and write a personal narrative.

> Write about a time when you tried to do something that was difficult but important to you. Tell what happened and why it mattered. Write for someone your own age. Include details and dialogue to help your readers picture and hear your experience.

Plan Use this chart to plan your narrative before you write.

| First event | detail: |
| | detail: |

| Second event | detail: |
| | detail: |

| Third event | detail: |
| | detail: |

Now write your personal narrative on the next page.   ➡

Copyright © Houghton Mifflin Company. All rights reserved.

Grade 4: Unit 8   Personal Narrative

Name _____

Writing a Personal Narrative *(continued from page 33)*

Write Your Personal Narrative Write your personal narrative based on the prompt on page 33. If you need more space, continue writing on another sheet of paper.

Remember to do these things to get a good score.

✔ Grab your readers' attention at the beginning.

✔ Use the pronoun *I*.

✔ Include only the important events, and tell them in order.

✔ Include details and dialogue that tell what you saw, heard, or felt.

✔ Write so that your narrative sounds like you.

✔ Tell how the experience worked out or how you felt at the end.

✔ Write complete sentences. Use what you have learned about capital letters, punctuation marks, and spelling. Use words correctly.

Number correct	15	16	17	18	19	20	21	22	23	24	25	26	27	28	29	30
Percent correct	50	53	57	60	63	67	70	73	77	80	83	87	90	93	97	100

Grade 4: Unit 8   Personal Narrative

Copyright © Houghton Mifflin Company. All rights reserved.

Name _____

Writing a Story

Revising 1–4. Revise the following paragraphs from a story, using the directions in the box. Use the space above each line, on the sides, and below the story for your changes.

- Write a beginning sentence that introduces the problem.
- Add a sentence to the first paragraph to make the story sound sadder.
- Take out a sentence that is not important to the story.
- Add one example of dialogue to show what a character thinks or feels.

The Tail Tells the Tale

Cory stopped in front of an old cocker spaniel's cage.

A sign said that his name was Brownie. Two rows away,

playful puppies leaped and yelped. They would have no

problem finding good homes.

"I want this old guy," said Cory.

Cory's mother said that she didn't agree.

Cory knelt in front of the old dog's cage and took a tennis

ball out of his pocket. Sure enough, Brownie's eyes lit up! He

dragged himself off the ground, and his tail began to wag.

Cory's mother smiled. She was very tall. "He's sort of cute

after all," she said. "Let's take Brownie home."

Copyright © Houghton Mifflin Company. All rights reserved.

Name _____

Writing a Story *(continued from page 35)*

Proofreading 5–10. Proofread the following paragraphs from a story to fix the six mistakes. Use proofreading marks to make your corrections.

- Find three mistakes in punctuating dialogue.
- Find one verb that doesn't agree with its subject.
- Find two misspelled words with the long *i* sound.

Proofreading Marks

¶   Indent
∧   Add
   Delete
≡   Capital letter
/   Small letter

A Batty Lesson

Did you remember to check the rabbit's water?" asked Dad.

Sarah shook her head. She stared at her book and tried to look

busy.

"Please go out to the shed rite now and check," said Dad.

"Take a flashlight", he added.

Sarah sighed. She hated going outsid at night! Sarah went

out back and ran across the lawn. Above her head, she heard

scary flapping sounds. "Bats!" she shouted. She raced for the

shed. Then Sarah sighed aloud, "You rabbits drinks a lot of

water, but I'll never forget to check it again!

Copyright © Houghton Mifflin Company. All rights reserved.

Name _____

Writing a Story *(continued from page 36)*

Writing Prompt: A Story 11–30. Follow the prompt below to plan and write a story.

> Write a story for someone your age about a character who moves to a new house and finds a secret passageway. Who is the character? Where does the passageway lead? What happens when the character follows the passageway?

Plan Use this story map to plan your story before you write.

Characters	Setting	Plot
		Beginning:
		Middle:
		End:

Now write your story on the next page.

Copyright © Houghton Mifflin Company. All rights reserved.

Grade 4: Unit 9   Story

Name _____

Writing a Story *(continued from page 37)*

Write Your Story Write your story based on the prompt on page 37. If you need more space, continue writing on another sheet of paper.

Remember to do these things to get a good score.

✔ Think of a plot with a beginning, a middle, and an end.

✔ Decide how your story will sound—scary? funny? serious? Choose details that help it sound this way.

✔ Introduce the main characters, the setting, and the problem in the beginning.

✔ In the middle, show how the characters deal with the problem. Tell only important events in an order that makes sense.

✔ Use details and dialogue to show rather than tell.

✔ In the end, tell how the problem works out.

✔ Write complete sentences. Use what you have learned about capital letters, punctuation marks, and spelling. Use words correctly.

_____

_____

_____

_____

_____

_____

_____

_____

_____

_____

_____

_____

Number correct	15	16	17	18	19	20	21	22	23	24	25	26	27	28	29	30
Percent correct	50	53	57	60	63	67	70	73	77	80	83	87	90	93	97	100

Grade 4: Unit 9   Story

Copyright © Houghton Mifflin Company. All rights reserved.

Name _____

Writing Instructions

Revising 1–4. Revise the following instructions, using the directions in the box. Use the space above each line, on the sides, and below the instructions for your changes.

> - Add the missing item to the sentence that lists the materials needed.
> - Take out the sentence that does not belong.
> - Add an order word.
> - Move a step that is out of order.

Coaxing Flowers into Spring

It's easy to coax spring flowers to bloom early. All you need are some pebbles and a few bulbs. Narcissus bulbs work well. You can find everything you need at a garden center. Our garden center has cute lawn ornaments!

Fill the bowl about half full of pebbles. Set the bowl in a sunny spot once you have followed all the steps. Then put the bulbs on top of the pebbles, about one inch apart. Fill the rest of the bowl with pebbles. Finally, add enough water to make the bottom of each bulb wet.

After four to six weeks, beautiful flowers will appear. You'll think spring has come early to your house!

Copyright © Houghton Mifflin Company. All rights reserved.

Name _____

Writing Instructions *(continued from page 39)*

Proofreading 5–10. Proofread this set of instructions to fix the six mistakes. Use proofreading marks to make your corrections.

> - Find two sentences that use two negatives together.
> - Find two missing commas.
> - Find two misspelled words with the long *o* sound.

Proofreading Marks

¶ Indent
∧ Add
‑ Delete
≡ Capital letter
/ Small letter

Make a Good Impression

How can you make great-looking cards signs, and invitations without spending a whole lot of money? Learn how to rubber-stamp.

First, look in a craft store where stamping supplies are sould. Find a rubber stamp that's right for your project. There are hundreds to choose from! In addition, you will need a colored ink pad some markers, and paper. You don't need no special kind of paper. Just make sure it's not shiny, or the ink won't stick.

When you're ready, cote the stamp with ink. Then press it down hard on a piece of paper. Don't never wiggle the stamp, or the design will blur. Finally, use markers to write messages around your design. The results are amazing! Everything you make will look store-bought.

Copyright © Houghton Mifflin Company. All rights reserved.

Grade 4: Unit 10   Instructions

Name _____

Writing Instructions *(continued from page 40)*

Writing Prompt: Instructions 11–30. Follow the prompt below to plan and write a set of instructions.

These pictures show how to make a wind chime. Look carefully at each picture. Then write instructions to go along with the pictures. Write for someone your age.

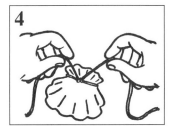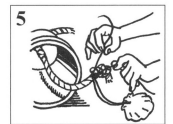

Plan Use this Step-by-Step Chart to plan your instructions before you write.

Steps	Materials Needed	Details

Now write your instructions on the next page.

Grade 4: Unit 10   Instructions

Copyright © Houghton Mifflin Company. All rights reserved.

Name _____

Writing Instructions *(continued from page 41)*

Write Your Instructions Write your instructions based on the prompt on page 41. If you need more space, continue writing on another sheet of paper.

Remember to do these things to get a good score.

✔ Begin with a topic sentence that tells what the instructions are about.
✔ Tell all the necessary materials.
✔ Include all the steps. Leave out anything that doesn't belong.
✔ Put the steps in the correct order. Use order words.
✔ Include exact details that make each step clear.
✔ Write a closing sentence that wraps up the instructions.
✔ Write complete sentences. Use what you have learned about capital letters, punctuation marks, and spelling. Use words correctly.

_____

_____

_____

_____

_____

_____

_____

_____

_____

_____

_____

_____

_____

Number correct	15	16	17	18	19	20	21	22	23	24	25	26	27	28	29	30
Percent correct	50	53	57	60	63	67	70	73	77	80	83	87	90	93	97	100

Copyright © Houghton Mifflin Company. All rights reserved.

Grade 4: Unit 10   Instructions

Name _____

Writing a Research Report

Revising 1–5. Revise the following paragraphs from a research report, using the directions in the box. Use the space above each line, on the sides, and below the report for your changes.

> • Rewrite the opening so that it is more interesting.
> • Add a topic sentence to the beginning of the third paragraph.
> • Take out two sentences that tell opinions rather than facts.
> • Add a closing sentence that sums up the ideas in the report.

The Water Boatman

Here's my report. It's about an insect called a water boatman.

It is easy to see how the water boatman got its name. Its body is shaped like a long, thin canoe, and its strong back legs stick out like oars. The water boatman has two breathing holes on its abdomen. These holes stick out of the water and allow the insect to breathe while swimming on its back. It's a pretty homely insect, if you ask me.

It gobbles up underwater insects. It also attacks and eats tadpoles and small fish. I feel badly for the cute little tadpoles! The water boatman grabs prey with its front legs. Then it kills the prey with poison from its mouth.

Copyright © Houghton Mifflin Company. All rights reserved.

Name _____

Writing a Research Report *(continued from page 43)*

Proofreading 6–10. Proofread these paragraphs from a research report to fix the five mistakes. Use proofreading marks to make your corrections.

- Find two mistakes in capitalization.
- Find one place where a new paragraph should begin.
- Find two misspelled words with the final |ər| sound.

Proofreading Marks

¶ Indent
∧ Add
⌒ Delete
≡ Capital letter
/ Small letter

An Actor's Life

In some ways, being an actor is like playing dress-up. In other ways, acting is much harder.

An actor has to make the story seem real. To do this, he or she must move and speak like someone else. A famous Russian acting teachor at the Onstage academy says that actors even need to *feel* their characters' emotions! Becoming an actor can take years of study. Acting students must learn how to run, walk, dance, sit, and fight on stage. They have to practice crying real tears and screaming with terrer. Acting students will often try many different kinds of drama, from plays by shakespeare to soap operas, before finding out which they do best.

➡

Copyright © Houghton Mifflin Company. All rights reserved.

Name _____

Writing a Research Report (continued from page 44)

Write a Paragraph for a Research Report 11–30. Write a paragraph for a research report about different forms of measurement, using the facts in the outline below.

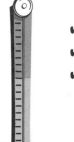
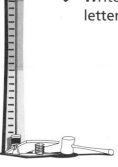

Remember to do these things to get a good score.

✔ Write a topic sentence that states the main idea.

✔ Use facts and details that support the main idea.

✔ Write complete sentences. Use what you have learned about capital letters, punctuation marks, and spelling. Use words correctly.

I. Early measurements
   A. A fathom—the distance between two outstretched arms—used to measure the depth of the sea
   B. A hand—the length of a human hand—used to measure the height of a horse
   C. A foot—a unit of distance—based on the length of a Roman soldier's foot
   D. A yard—a unit of distance—the length of England's King Henry I's arm

_____

_____

_____

_____

_____

_____

_____

_____

_____

Number correct	15	16	17	18	19	20	21	22	23	24	25	26	27	28	29	30
Percent correct	50	53	57	60	63	67	70	73	77	80	83	87	90	93	97	100

Grade 4: Unit 11   Research Report

Copyright © Houghton Mifflin Company. All rights reserved.

Writing to Express an Opinion

Revising 1–4. Revise the following paragraphs from an opinion essay, using the directions in the box. Use the space above each line, on the sides, and below the essay for your changes.

> • Rewrite the opening so that the topic of the essay is clear.
> • Move one sentence that is out of place.
> • Write a sentence to elaborate the final reason in the second paragraph.
> • Write a topic sentence for the third paragraph.

Hot Season, Cool Camp

My town is interesting. There are lots of camps nearby—
Red Hill, Pine Knoll, Salt Meadow.

It's hard to say what I like most about Red Hill Camp. I really enjoy learning about nature. I love splashing through the muddy pond and finding lime green frogs! Then, after the rain, swarms of mosquitoes by the pond can ruin the canoeing. Another thing I like is that you make new friends. Last year, I ended up hanging around with different kids from those I hung out with at school. Finally, the food in the dining hall is delicious!

On hot days, the three-mile hikes feel way too long. On rainy days, we can't play outside. Some mornings, when I hear my alarm ring at 7:00 A.M., I feel like just staying in bed.

Copyright © Houghton Mifflin Company. All rights reserved.

Name _____

Writing to Express an Opinion *(continued from page 47)*

Proofreading 5–10. Proofread the following paragraphs from an opinion essay to fix the six mistakes. Use proofreading marks to make your corrections.

- Find two places where a pronoun doesn't agree with the noun it replaces.
- Find two mistakes in forming contractions.
- Find two misspelled words with suffixes.

Proofreading Marks	
¶	Indent
∧	Add
℘	Delete
≡	Capital letter
/	Small letter

Highway Ups and Downs

Each year when our family drives four hundred miles to Chicago, my sister and I groan. We girls do'nt like going because long car trips bore us. Every hour seems endles! We can't read because w'ell start to feel carsick. We get stiff and uncomfortable. Also, we argue over the radio. Should they be on an AM or an FM station? How high should the volume be?

These trips have their good points, however. We play word games and spot license plates. In addition, my parents pack great surprises, such as snacks and playing cards. You let us bring along our favorite tapes too. Then there's the most wonderfull part of all—arriving at our destination!

Copyright © Houghton Mifflin Company. All rights reserved.

Name _____

Writing to Express an Opinion *(continued from page 48)*

Writing Prompt: An Opinion Essay 11–30. Follow the prompt below to plan and write an opinion essay.

> Write an opinion essay about the place where you live. Tell someone who is your age what you like and don't like about living in that location.

Plan Use the clusters below to plan your essay before you write. Use both clusters, one for the things you like and one for the things you don't like.

Opinion — reason — detail
detail
detail

Opinion — reason — detail
detail
detail

Now write your opinion essay on the next page. ➡

Copyright © Houghton Mifflin Company. All rights reserved.

Grade 4: Unit 12   Opinion

Writing to Express an Opinion *(continued from page 49)*

Write Your Opinion Essay Write your opinion essay based on the prompt on page 49. If you need more space, continue writing on another sheet of paper.

Remember to do these things to get a good score.

✔ Introduce your topic in the opening. Say something that will hook your audience right away.

✔ For each paragraph, write a topic sentence that tells the main idea.

✔ Include strong reasons to support your opinion.

✔ Use details, such as examples, to explain each reason.

✔ Write in a way that sounds like you.

✔ Sum up the important points in the closing.

✔ Write complete sentences. Use what you have learned about capital letters, punctuation marks, and spelling. Use words correctly.

_____

_____

_____

_____

_____

_____

_____

_____

_____

_____

_____

_____

_____

_____

_____

_____

Copyright © Houghton Mifflin Company. All rights reserved.

Number correct	15	16	17	18	19	20	21	22	23	24	25	26	27	28	29	30
Percent correct	50	53	57	60	63	67	70	73	77	80	83	87	90	93	97	100

Name _____

Writing to Persuade

Revising 1–4. Revise the following paragraph from a persuasive essay, using the directions in the box. Use the space above each line, on the sides, and below the narrative for your changes.

- Write an opening sentence that states the goal of the essay.
- Write a topic sentence for the second paragraph.
- Find the supporting sentence that tells an opinion. Rewrite it as a fact or an example.
- Write a closing sentence that sums up the goal and the reasons.

Say Yes to Uniforms!

First, school uniforms would be good for students. The uniform would remind students that they are at school to do a job. Students would fool around less and study more. If all students at school dressed the same, they would feel more like part of a group. It's dumb that only some lucky kids get to wear the expensive, trendy clothes.

Parents would know just where to buy school clothes. They could save money by passing uniforms from child to child because the uniforms would always be in fashion. There would be fewer arguments between parents and children about what's okay to wear to school.

Copyright © Houghton Mifflin Company. All rights reserved.

Name _____

Writing to Persuade *(continued from page 51)*

Proofreading 5–10. Proofread the following paragraph from a persuasive essay to fix the six mistakes. Use proofreading marks to make your corrections.

- Find two mistakes with making comparisons with adverbs.
- Find two mistakes in forming possessive nouns.
- Find two misspelled words with the |ôr| sound.

Proofreading Marks

¶	Indent
∧	Add
℘	Delete
≡	Capital letter
/	Small letter

From Basement to Family Fun Center

Let's turn our dusty old basement into a family fun center!

With one central place for all of the kids stuff, the rest of the

house would stay cleaner. Jasons band could practice in the

fun center instead of in the kitchen. I would study a lot hardest

than I do now if I had a place to spread out and work. Of all

three kids, little Tina plays the louder! If we had a fun center,

she could ride her tricycle, gallop around on her toy horse, and

rore like a lion without disturbing anybody. Fore peace and

quiet in the rest of the house, we need a family fun center.

Copyright © Houghton Mifflin Company. All rights reserved.

Writing to Persuade (continued from page 52)

Writing Prompt: A Persuasive Essay 11–30. Follow the prompt below to plan and write a persuasive essay.

> Think about a club or an activity that you would like to join. Write an essay to persuade a parent or other adult to allow you to join.

Plan Use this web to plan your essay before you write.

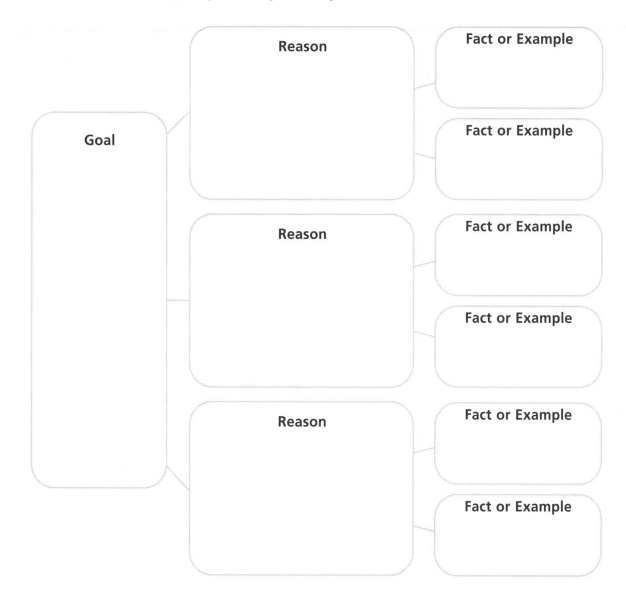

Goal

Reason — Fact or Example / Fact or Example

Reason — Fact or Example / Fact or Example

Reason — Fact or Example / Fact or Example

Now write your persuasive essay on the next page. ➡

Copyright © Houghton Mifflin Company. All rights reserved.

Name _____

Writing to Persuade (continued from page 53)

Write Your Persuasive Essay Write your persuasive essay based on the prompt on page 53. If you need more space, continue writing on another sheet of paper.

Remember to do these things to get a good score.

✔ In the opening, state your goal clearly and simply. Tell your audience what you want them to do.

✔ Give strong reasons to support your goal. Back up your reasons with facts and examples.

✔ Tell your reasons from most important to least important.

✔ Use a confident, positive voice.

✔ In the closing, sum up your reasons, and call your audience to action.

✔ Write complete sentences. Use what you have learned about capital letters, punctuation marks, and spelling. Use words correctly.

_____

_____

_____

_____

_____

_____

_____

_____

_____

_____

_____

_____

_____

_____

Number correct	15	16	17	18	19	20	21	22	23	24	25	26	27	28	29	30
Percent correct	50	53	57	60	63	67	70	73	77	80	83	87	90	93	97	100

Grade 4: Unit 13   Persuasion

Copyright © Houghton Mifflin Company. All rights reserved.

Name _____

Unit 1: The Sentence

Sentences If a group of words below is a sentence, write it correctly. If it is not, write *not a sentence*.

1. the blizzard lasted all night

   _____

2. did you look outside in the morning

   _____

3. was covered with snow

   _____

Subjects and Predicates Draw a line between the complete subject and the complete predicate. Then underline each simple subject once and each simple predicate twice.

4. My younger brother plays the violin.

5. His music teacher gives lessons after school.

6. The students in the class tune their instruments.

Run-on Sentences Rewrite each run-on sentence correctly.

7. The dragon opened its jaws a flame shot out.

   _____

8. A princess came out of the castle, she turned on a hose.

   _____

9. The dragon ran away the princess grinned.

   _____

Unit 2: Nouns

Kinds of Nouns Underline each noun. Then write each proper noun correctly.

10. His sister goes to a college in michigan. _____

11. The doctor gave aunt nancy some medicine. _____

12. Our town celebrates may day at emerson park. _____

Copyright © Houghton Mifflin Company. All rights reserved.

Name _____

Unit 2: Nouns (continued from page 55)

Singular and Plural Nouns Write the plural of each noun.

13. kiss _____

16. discovery _____

14. woman _____

17. peach _____

15. donkey _____

18. tooth _____

Possessive Nouns Write each group of words another way. Use the possessive form of each underlined noun.

19. tail of a <u>cat</u> _____

20. tools owned by <u>carpenters</u> _____

21. store for <u>women</u> _____

Unit 3: Verbs

Main and Helping Verbs Draw one line under the main verb and two lines under the helping verb.

22. They were trying their best.

24. The summer was coming to an end.

23. Tanya had discovered the answer.

25. Moths will eat holes in a sweater.

Present, Past, and Future Underline the verb in each sentence. Then write *present, past,* or *future.*

26. A loud car horn startled me. _____

27. That rubber barrel catches the rain. _____

28. I will practice my piano piece later tonight. _____

Agreement and Spelling the Present Tense Write the correct present-tense form of the verb in ( ). If it is correct as it is, write *correct.*

29. Gabriel (sing) with the chorus every Sunday. _____

30. My rabbit's nose often (twitch) nervously. _____

31. We (remember) the way to your apartment building. _____

32. That silver trailer (carry) two champion horses. _____

Copyright © Houghton Mifflin Company. All rights reserved.

Name _____

Unit 3: Verbs (continued from page 56)

Past Tense and the Past with Helping Verbs Underline the correct verb form in ( ).

33. My sister (taped, tapped) politely on my bedroom door.

34. The farmers (worried, worryed) about dry weather.

35. I (has, have) solved the problem at last!

36. Marissa has (threw, thrown) two strikes and a ball.

37. Our class (sang, sung) "America the Beautiful" at the assembly.

The Special Verb *be* Underline the correct form of the verb *be* in ( ).

38. I (is, am)   40. people (was, were)   42. winter (was, were)

39. you (was, were)   41. Jake (is, are)   43. they (is, are)

Contractions with *not* Write the contractions for the following words.

44. could not _____   46. will not _____

45. have not _____   47. does not _____

Unit 4: Adjectives

Adjectives Underline each adjective. Circle the noun it describes. Do not underline *a, an,* and *the.*

48. I saw a strange flower.   50. They were red and pink.

49. It had five huge petals.   51. The stem was fuzzy.

Using *a, an,* and *the* Underline the correct article in ( ).

52. (a, an) airplane   53. (an, the) ice cubes   54. (a, an) number

Comparisons Write the correct form of the adjective in ( ).

55. Donelle was the (happy) girl in the class! _____

56. This slice of bacon is (thin) than that one. _____

57. The old chair is (comfortable) than the new one. _____

58. That was the (bad) vacation I have ever taken. _____

59. The plum is (good) than the pear. _____

Copyright © Houghton Mifflin Company. All rights reserved.

Name _____

Unit 5: Capitalization and Punctuation

Correct Sentences Write these sentences correctly.

60. what gorgeous apples those are how many shall we get

_____

61. my brother is taking me to the movies would you like to come

_____

62. do you like cheese pizza with onions help yourself to a slice

_____

Proper Nouns and Titles Find the proper nouns and the titles in these sentences. Write them correctly.

63. On monday, dr. emeka omaliko will arrive from nigeria.

_____

64. I think bingo chewed up my favorite magazine, american girl.

_____

65. What a great time I had with grandfather on new year's day!

_____

66. My aunt went to barton books and bought me a book called mystery in the mirror.

_____

Abbreviations Write an abbreviation for each word.

67. Junior _____   70. Avenue _____

68. Tuesday _____   71. September _____

69. Doctor _____   72. January _____

Commas Add commas where they are needed.

73. Gulls swans and ducks are all birds that can swim.

74. Did you see the weather report on TV Charlotte?

75. Yes it predicted rain and sleet.

76. The problem Mom is that I can't find my boots.

Copyright © Houghton Mifflin Company. All rights reserved.

Unit 5: Capitalization and Punctuation (continued from page 58)

Quotations Rewrite the following sentences. Add punctuation marks and capital letters where they are needed. If a sentence is fine as it is, write *correct*.

77. where are you going with those pots and pans asked Amalia.

_____

78. Niko answered we're going to a parade for Groundhog Day.

_____

79. Amalia asked what the pots and pans were for.

_____

80. everyone bangs on them to wake the groundhog replied Niko.

_____

Unit 6: Pronouns

Subject, Object, and Possessive Pronouns Replace each underlined word or words with the correct pronoun.

81. <u>John</u> climbed into the canoe. _____

82. John pushed <u>John's</u> canoe away from the bank. _____

83. John waved to <u>Mother and Father</u>. _____

84. His mother called to <u>John</u>, "Be careful!" _____

85. The parents got into <u>the parents'</u> car and drove off. _____

I and *me* and **Homophones** Underline the word or words that complete each sentence correctly.

86. (Your, You're) a good in-line skater.

87. Mrs. Brown thanked (James and I, James and me) for helping her.

88. (Ellie and me, Ellie and I) take the same bus to school.

89. All of the students put (their, there) backpacks in the closet.

90. Will you play basketball with (me and Sean, Sean and me)?

91. A raccoon stuck (it's, its) nose into the garbage can.

Copyright © Houghton Mifflin Company. All rights reserved.

Name _____

Unit 6: Pronouns *(continued from page 59)*

Contractions with Pronouns Write the contraction for each of the following words.

92. we are _____

94. you will _____

93. I have _____

95. I am _____

Unit 7: Adverbs and Prepositions

What Is an Adverb? Underline each adverb. Circle the verb it describes.

96. Tyler sang the song sweetly.

98. A scared kitten ran inside.

97. I finally found my favorite cap.

99. Now I understand this math problem.

Comparing with Adverbs Write the correct form of the adverb in ( ).

100. Can you see the star that shines (clearly) of all?

_____

101. Juno writes (fast) than I do. _____

102. Of all the dogs, the spaniel jumped (high). _____

103. Charles behaves (politely) than his brother. _____

Using *good* and *well* and Negatives Underline the correct word to complete each sentence.

104. I haven't (ever, never) skied.

106. We don't have (any, no) paper.

105. Stir the soup (good, well).

107. She learned her lesson (good, well).

What Is a Preposition? Draw one line under each prepositional phrase and two lines under each preposition.

108. The ball dropped through the basket.

109. Roberto was resting on a park bench.

110. I can hardly wait until Saturday.

Number correct	55	56	57	58	59	60	61	62	63	64	65	66	67	68	69	70	71	72	73	74
Percent correct	50	51	52	52	53	54	55	56	57	58	59	60	61	62	62	63	64	65	66	67

Number correct	75	76	77	78	79	80	81	82	83	84	85	86	87	88	89	90	91	92	93	94
Percent correct	68	69	70	71	72	72	73	74	75	76	77	78	79	80	81	82	82	83	84	85

Number correct	95	96	97	98	99	100	101	102	103	104	105	106	107	108	109	110
Percent correct	86	87	88	89	90	91	92	92	93	94	95	96	97	98	99	100

Copyright © Houghton Mifflin Company. All rights reserved.

Grade 4: End-of-Year Grammar Test

Copyright © Houghton Mifflin Company. All rights reserved.

Name _____

Writing a Description

Write a Description 1–20. Look at the picture of the ice-cream cone. Write a description of it for someone your age. Describe how it looks, feels, and tastes.

Plan Before you write, plan your description. Label each detail in the following list with the word *looks*, *sounds*, *feels*, or *tastes* to show what sense or senses that detail describes. Then fill in the chart by writing each detail in the correct column. Sample details are shown.

dark brown cone	_____looks_____
swirl of pale pink	_____looks_____
crisp crunch against teeth	_____feels, sounds_____
last bit of cone like damp cardboard	_____feels_____
sharp tang of fresh strawberry	_____tastes_____
soothing, creamy softness	_____feels_____
sugary sweetness	_____tastes_____
sprinkles dotted like bits of confetti	_____looks_____

	Ice-cream Cone		
Looks	**Sounds**	**Feels**	**Tastes**
dark brown cone	crisp crunch against teeth	crisp crunch against teeth	sharp tang of fresh strawberry
swirl of pale pink		last bit of cone like damp cardboard	sugary sweetness
sprinkles dotted like bits of confetti		soothing, creamy softness	

Write your description on the next page.

Grade 4: Getting Started: The Writing Process

Copyright © Houghton Mifflin Company. All rights reserved.

Name _____

Writing a Description (continued from page 1)

Write Your Description Write a description of the ice-cream cone shown in the picture on page 1. Beginning and ending sentences are given below. Use the details in your chart to write supporting sentences that describe the ice-cream cone. Use exact words, and elaborate your sentences to make your description clear and vivid. Sample description is shown.

I will never get tired of strawberry ice-cream cones. I start to drool the minute I see the tall swirl of pale pink above the dark brown cone. Sometimes I order sprinkles, and they dot the ice cream like little bits of confetti.

I take the first bite and feel the soothing, creamy softness of the ice cream, followed by the crisp crunch of the cone against my teeth. The sharp tang of fresh strawberry tickles my taste buds, but it's mixed with sugary sweetness. I eat as slowly as possible. Finally, I eat the last bit of cone, which has soaked up so much melting ice cream that it feels like damp cardboard.

_____

_____

_____

_____

_____

_____

_____

After I lick my lips, I start dreaming of the next time I'll place the same order.

Number correct 10 11 12 13 14 15 16 17 18 19 20
Percent correct 50 55 60 65 70 75 80 85 90 95 100

Grade 4: Getting Started: The Writing Process

Name _____

The Sentence

What Is a Sentence? Underline each group of words that is a sentence.

1. We took our bikes to the park.
2. Locked them carefully.
3. The old, broken swings.
4. Joe went down the slide.

Statements and Questions; Commands and Exclamations Write each sentence correctly.

5. please open the window **Please open the window.**
6. will you help me **Will you help me?**
7. what a mess they made **What a mess they made!**
8. we should clean it up **We should clean it up.**
9. where shall we start **Where shall we start?**
10. pick up those toys **Pick up those toys. / Pick up those toys!**

Subjects and Predicates Draw a line between each complete subject and complete predicate.

11. Pandas | are not really bears.
12. My family | saw two pandas at the National Zoo.
13. Both furry animals | played.

Simple Subjects The complete subject of each sentence is underlined. Circle each simple subject.

14. My older (sister) uses Dad's home computer.
15. (Sharon) solves problems with it.
16. Some (friends) of mine have their own computers.
17. The (keyboard) of the computer is easily broken.

Copyright © Houghton Mifflin Company. All rights reserved.

Name _____

The Sentence (continued from page 3)

Simple Predicates The complete predicate of each sentence is underlined. Circle each simple predicate.

18. I (spilled) apple juice on the keyboard last week.
19. Dad (hollered).
20. He (has) another computer at his office, though.
21. Sharon's friend (uses) the computer often.
22. She and I (play) computer games.

Correcting Run-on Sentences Rewrite each run-on sentence correctly.

23. The air was cold we built a fire.
The air was cold. We built a fire.
24. Our tent leaked, we patched the holes.
Our tent leaked. We patched the holes.

Proofreading 25–32. Proofread the paragraphs below. Correct the five mistakes in punctuation and three mistakes in capital letters.
Example: I just saw my first tuatara. what an interesting animal it is!

The tuatara is the oldest, coldest, and slowest of all reptiles? It has lived on Earth for nearly two hundred million years. This animal is found on a few tiny islands in New Zealand. It lives in the nests of sea birds. The male can be over two feet long, but the female is shorter both can live as long as seventy years.

Temperatures as low as 45°F are quite comfortable for this reptile. It breathes only about once an hour one or two earthworms a week satisfy its hunger.

The tuatara has three eyes. The third eye cannot see objects, but it can tell light from dark. What a strange animal this is /!

Copyright © Houghton Mifflin Company. All rights reserved.

Copyright © Houghton Mifflin Company. All rights reserved.

Name _____

The Sentence *(continued from page 4)*

The Sentence 33–40. Read each passage below and find the numbered, underlined parts. Choose the answer that shows the best way to capitalize and punctuate each underlined part. Fill in the circle next to that answer.

Which bus did you take? On the
_____
              (33)
field trip? We were on Bus 4. What a

disaster that was the air-conditioning
_____
              (34)
broke down? a girl got sick and a boy
_____
              (35)
got a bloody nose. Then the bus got a
_____
              (36)
flat tire.

33. Ⓐ take? on
Ⓑ take. On
Ⓒ take on
Ⓓ Correct as it is

34. Ⓕ was! The
Ⓖ was? the
Ⓗ was! the
Ⓙ Correct as it is

35. Ⓐ down a
Ⓑ down. a
Ⓒ down. A
Ⓓ Correct as it is

36. Ⓕ nose? Then
Ⓖ nose. then
Ⓗ nose then
Ⓙ Correct as it is

Have you ever been to the

seashore? have you ever seen an animal
_____
              (37)
walking sideways across the sand. This
_____
              (38)
creature is called a crab a crab is an
_____
              (39)
animal with a jointed shell and ten

legs The front legs end in big claws.
_____
              (40)

37. Ⓐ seashore. Have
Ⓑ seashore! Have
Ⓒ seashore? Have
Ⓓ Correct as it is

38. Ⓕ sand. this
Ⓖ sand this
Ⓗ sand? This
Ⓙ Correct as it is

39. Ⓐ crab! a
Ⓑ crab. A
Ⓒ crab? a
Ⓓ Correct as it is

40. Ⓕ legs. The
Ⓖ legs. the
Ⓗ legs? The
Ⓙ Correct as it is

Number correct 20 21 22 23 24 25 26 27 28 29 30 31 32 33 34 35 36 37 38 39 40
Percent correct 50 53 55 58 60 63 65 68 70 73 75 78 80 83 85 88 90 93 95 98 100

Grade 4: Unit 1 The Sentence

5

Copyright © Houghton Mifflin Company. All rights reserved.

Name _____

Nouns

What Is a Noun? Underline the nouns in each sentence.

1. The store had a big sale.
2. Stan has saved his money.
3. The price of skates is low now.
4. The ice on the pond has melted.

Common and Proper Nouns Write the common and the proper nouns from each sentence. Use capital letters correctly in the proper nouns.

5. The twins live in new mexico. **twins, New Mexico**
6. Uncle hank is coming for thanksgiving. **Uncle Hank, Thanksgiving**
7. Is dania sanchez interested in the planets? **Dania Sanchez, planets**
8. My sister is a teacher in miami, florida. **sister, teacher, Miami, Florida**

Singular and Plural Nouns Underline the correct noun in (). If it is singular, write S. If it is plural, write P.

9. This (pet, pets) needs a lot of care. **S**
10. Liat cleaned both (cage, cages). **P**
11. Her hamsters play in several (box, boxes). **P**
12. Bill feeds his dog two (sandwich, sandwiches) for lunch. **P**
13. Yesterday he took the dog on a (bus, buses). **S**

Nouns Ending with y Complete each sentence with the plural form of the noun in ().

14. This hotel has two **lobbies** . (lobby)
15. The desk clerk found the **keys** to our rooms. (key)
16. Three **flies** were buzzing outside the window. (fly)
17. Room service brought a dish of **strawberries** . (strawberry)

Copyright © Houghton Mifflin Company. All rights reserved.

Name _____

Nouns (continued from page 7)

More Plural Nouns Complete each sentence with the plural form of the noun in ().

18. A pair of **oxen** pulled the heavy wagon. (ox)
19. The **children** helped with the animals. (child)
20. Our cat chased two **mice** in the barn. (mouse)
21. The dog rounded up the **sheep** . (sheep)

Singular Possessive Nouns Write each group of words another way. Use the possessive form of each underlined noun.

22. dish that the dog uses — **the dog's dish**
23. spaceship of Rexdar — **Rexdar's spaceship**
24. car belonging to the woman — **the woman's car**
25. name of the baby — **the baby's name**

Plural Possessive Nouns Complete each group of words with the possessive form of the noun in ().

26. the **monkeys'** cages (monkeys)
27. the **armies'** supplies (armies)
28. the **sheep's** wool (sheep)
29. the **lizards'** lungs (lizards)

Copyright © Houghton Mifflin Company. All rights reserved.

Copyright © Houghton Mifflin Company. All rights reserved.

Name _____

Nouns (continued from page 8)

Proofreading 30–37. Proofread the paragraphs below. Find one incorrect proper noun, four incorrect plural nouns, and three incorrect possessive nouns. Correct the mistakes.

Example: The ~~mayors'~~ office is in the town hall.   **mayor's**

> **Vicky's**
> ~~Vickys'~~ father is the mayor of our town. Mr. Wade always
> performs his ~~dutys~~ with a cheerful smile. The ~~childs~~ in our   **duties** **children**
> school look forward to his visits. He often gives us little ~~toyes~~.   **toys**
> He makes funny ~~speechs~~ too.   **speeches**
> Mr. Wade also sells ~~mens'~~ shoes in his store near Glen ~~park~~.   **men's** **P**
>
> In the window of his store, a large photograph shows Mr.
> Wade's sons dressed up as turkeys for Thanksgiving. The ~~boys~~   **boys'**
> feathers are orange and black.

9

Copyright © Houghton Mifflin Company. All rights reserved.

Name _____

Nouns (continued from page 9)

Nouns 38–45. Choose the best way to write the underlined part of each sentence. Fill in the circle beside that answer. If there is no mistake, fill in the circle beside the last answer.

38. Elena's birthday is on <u>Flag Day</u>.
Ⓐ flag day
Ⓑ Flag day
Ⓒ flag Day
Ⓓ (No mistakes) ●

39. Our new <u>Dog is named bo</u>.
Ⓕ dog is named Bo ●
Ⓖ dog is named bo
Ⓗ Dog is named Bo
Ⓙ (No mistakes)

40. Movers packed fifty <u>boxs</u>.
Ⓐ boxies
Ⓑ box
Ⓒ boxes ●
Ⓓ (No mistakes)

41. The television show was about a family of <u>monkey</u>.
Ⓕ monkees
Ⓖ monkeys ●
Ⓗ monkies
Ⓙ (No mistakes)

42. Two <u>woman</u> demonstrated karate for the students.
Ⓐ women ●
Ⓑ womans
Ⓒ womens
Ⓓ (No mistakes)

43. Several <u>factories</u> were closed down.
Ⓕ factory
Ⓖ factorys
Ⓗ factory's
Ⓙ (No mistakes) ●

44. <u>Susans'</u> toothpaste tastes like cinnamon.
Ⓐ Susans
Ⓑ Susan's ●
Ⓒ Susan'
Ⓓ (No mistakes)

45. All of the <u>mens</u> jackets are on sale.
Ⓕ mens'
Ⓖ menses'
Ⓗ men's ●
Ⓙ (No mistakes)

Number correct	22	23	24	25	26	27	28	29	30	31	32	33	34	35	36	37	38	39	40	41
Percent correct	49	51	53	56	58	60	62	64	67	69	71	73	76	78	80	82	84	87	89	91

Number correct	42	43	44	45
Percent correct	93	96	98	100

10

Name _____

Verbs

Action Verbs Underline the action verb in each sentence.

1. Fred prepared a pie.
2. First, he mixed the crust.
3. Sue helped him.
4. Sue peeled a dozen apples.
5. The oven made a funny noise.
6. The pie baked for forty minutes.

Main Verbs and Helping Verbs Underline the helping verb in each sentence. Circle the main verb.

7. We had (waited) for you at the fairgrounds.
8. Yolanda is (showing) her prize pig.
9. The dog has (slept) under a tree.
10. The band will (play) three songs.
11. I am (leaving) for home now.

Present, Past, and Future Underline the verb in each sentence. Then write *present, past,* or *future.*

12. We chatted about the weather. _____ **past**
13. Yesterday it rained all morning. _____ **past**
14. Snow will fall Friday. _____ **future**
15. Usually the wind blows from the south. _____ **present**
16. The sun will shine this weekend. _____ **future**

Subject-Verb Agreement Underline the correct verb form in ( ).

17. Pigs (eat, eats) turnips.
18. The farmer (plant, plants) turnips in July.
19. In November he (harvest, harvests) them.
20. Mom and Dad (enjoy, enjoys) mashed turnips.

Copyright © Houghton Mifflin Company. All rights reserved.

Name _____

Verbs *(continued from page 11)*

Spelling the Present Tense Write the present tense of the verb in ( ).

21. Our leaky radiator **worries** us. (worry)
22. A bucket **catches** the water. (catch)
23. The bucket **overflows** often. (overflow)
24. Our neighbor, Rusty, **fixes** the leak from time to time. (fix)

Spelling the Past Tense Write the past tense of the verb in ( ).

25. Mr. Drummond **employed** Doug and Marcy. (employ)
26. Together, they **copied** Mr. Drummond's papers. (copy)
27. Doug **liked** his job. (like)
28. He **hummed** in the elevator. (hum)

The Past with Helping Verbs Write *have* or *has* to complete each sentence correctly.

29. The students **have** practiced the song.
30. Lamont **has** played it on his guitar.
31. Our teacher **has** planned a concert.
32. We **have** helped her.

Irregular Verbs Write the correct past form of the verb in ( ).

33. Rocky and Louie have **begun** a garden. (begin)
34. Last year they **grew** tomatoes. (grow)
35. The year before they had **grown** corn and beans. (grow)
36. Louie almost **broke** the shovel. (break)

Copyright © Houghton Mifflin Company. All rights reserved.

Copyright © Houghton Mifflin Company. All rights reserved.

Unit 3 Test

Name _____

Verbs *(continued from page 12)*

The Special Verb *be* Underline the correct form of the verb *be* in ( ).

37. The girls (is, **are**) sisters.

38. Last year I (**was**, were) in their math class.

39. They (was, **were**) good students.

40. Math (**is**, are) still their favorite subject.

Contractions with *not* Write a contraction to replace the underlined word or words.

41. Wild gorillas <u>do not</u> live in North America. **don't**

42. Gorillas <u>are not</u> strong swimmers. **aren't**

43. Apes <u>cannot</u> eat unripe fruit. **can't**

44. Adult female gorillas <u>will not</u> groom each other. **won't**

45. Hunters <u>should not</u> kill gorillas for their skins. **shouldn't**

Proofreading 46–52. Proofread the paragraphs below. Find one incorrect contraction and six incorrect verb forms. Correct the mistakes.

Example: I ~~has~~ enjoyed my pet indri, a kind of mammal related to the monkey. **have**

My indri's name is Brat, and he looks like a little white monkey. He comes
from an island in the Indian Ocean. Sometimes Brat ~~clutchs~~ my hand, and **clutches**
sometimes he walks alone. He ~~steadys~~ himself with his long, slender arms. Still, **steadies**
he ~~have~~ tripped once or twice. **has**

Yesterday morning at six o'clock, Brat ~~hoped~~ up onto my bed. He was **hopped**
hungry. I was still very sleepy, but Brat ~~would'nt~~ leave me alone! I gave him **wouldn't**
some tender leaves for his breakfast. All too soon, Brat had ~~ate~~ enough, and he **eaten**
wanted his bath. I grumbled a little, but then I washed him in the sink. Next, I
~~dryed~~ him with a face cloth. Brat was clean, fluffy, and ready for more fun! **dried**

Grade 4: Unit 3 Verbs

13

Copyright © Houghton Mifflin Company. All rights reserved.

Unit 3 Test

Name _____

Verbs *(continued from page 13)*

Verbs 53–60. Read each passage. Choose the line that shows the mistake. Fill in the circle beside that answer. If there is no mistake, fill in the circle beside the last answer.

53. (A) Max has growed.
    (B) He can't fit into his jacket anymore.
    (C) Yesterday he wore a sweater.
    (D) (No mistakes)

54. (F) Last year Cristina collects shells. Now she collects fans.
    (G) Luckily she has a big room!
    (H)
    (J) (No mistakes)

55. (A) An owl lives near our house.
    (B) It screechs so loudly at night!
    (C) Last night it drove me crazy.
    (D) (No mistakes)

56. (F) My baby cousins is cute. Philip
    (G) sits and watches everybody.
    (H) Henri doesn't sit still at all.
    (J) (No mistakes)

57. (A) Tomorrow, Walker will give
    (B) a piano recital. He plays well.
    (C) He have studied for many years.
    (D) (No mistakes)

58. (F) Dad took me to the bowling
    (G) alley on Monday. I threw the ball
    (H) so badly. I dont ever improve!
    (J) (No mistakes)

59. (A) The storm began at noon.
    (B) After the rain stoped, we went
    (C) outside. We took a long walk.
    (D) (No mistakes)

60. (F) I am baking a carrot cake.
    (G) The oven timer buzzes loudly.
    (H) The cake is'nt done yet.
    (J) (No mistakes)

Number correct	30	31	32	33	34	35	36	37	38	39	40	41	42	43	44	45	46	47	48	49
Percent correct	50	52	53	55	57	58	60	62	63	65	67	68	70	72	73	75	77	78	80	82
Number correct	50	51	52	53	54	55	56	57	58	59	60
Percent correct	83	85	87	89	90	92	93	95	97	98	100

Grade 4: Unit 3 Verbs

14

Name _____

Adjectives

What Is an Adjective? Underline each adjective. Circle the noun it describes. Do not underline *a* and *the*.

1. The frisky, new (puppy) tumbled in the grass.

2. It saw two busy (bees) in the garden.

3. The playful (puppy) chased after the bees.

4. Soon the puppy had a sore (nose) from a nasty (sting).

Adjectives After *be* Underline each adjective that comes after a form of the verb *be*. Circle the word it describes.

5. Some (movies) are exciting.

6. That (film) was dull though.

7. Even the (popcorn) was stale!

8. My (neck) is stiff.

9. Sometimes (I) am cranky.

10. (Julie) was noisy during the movie.

Using *a*, *an*, and *the* Underline the correct article in ( ).

11. We found (a, an) strange thing in (an, the) garage.

12. It was (a, an) oil painting of (a, an) wooded scene.

13. (A, The) painting was dusty but not torn.

14. (A, An) old painting can be (a, an) valuable find!

Making Comparisons Write the correct form of the adjective in ( ).

15. In Iowa, July is the __**hottest**__ month of the year. (hot)

16. This is the __**warmest**__ day ever. (warm)

17. Yesterday was __**sunnier**__ than today. (sunny)

18. This thunderstorm is __**closer**__ than the one last week. (close)

⬆

Grade 4: Unit 4   Adjectives

Copyright © Houghton Mifflin Company. All rights reserved.

Name _____

Adjectives *(continued from page 15)*

Comparing with *more* and *most* Write the correct form of the adjective in ( ).

19. This event is __**more exciting**__ than Columbus Day. (exciting)

20. Pearl has the __**most unusual**__ costume of all. (unusual)

21. She is dressed as the __**most mysterious**__ princess in Idaho. (mysterious)

22. Her hat is even __**more fantastic**__ than her outfit. (fantastic)

Comparing with *good* and *bad* Write the correct form of the word in ( ).

23. The __**better**__ painting of the two will take the prize. (good)

24. My painting style is __**worse**__ than Kaye's. (bad)

25. The __**worst**__ part of the whole contest is the judging. (bad)

26. Winning is the __**best**__ feeling of all. (good)

⬆

Copyright © Houghton Mifflin Company. All rights reserved.

Grade 4: Unit 4   Adjectives

Copyright © Houghton Mifflin Company. All rights reserved.

Name _____

Adjectives (continued from page 17)

Adjectives 35–40. Look at each underlined part of the paragraph. Find the correct way to write the underlined part in each numbered line. Fill in the circle beside that answer. If the part is already correct, fill in the circle beside the last answer, "Correct as it is."

(35) One of the <u>scaryest</u> things in the world is

(36) an earthquake. Even the <u>smallest</u> quake feels odd.

(37) A <u>biger</u> one is terrifying! One of the world's

(38) <u>worse</u> quakes struck Los Angeles in 1994.

(39) An even <u>badder</u> quake rocked Japan in 1923.

(40) The <u>terriblest</u> earthquakes can destroy whole towns.

35. Ⓐ scarier
Ⓑ most scaryest
Ⓒ scariest
Ⓓ Correct as it is

36. Ⓕ smalest
Ⓖ smaller
Ⓗ most small
Ⓙ Correct as it is

37. Ⓐ bigger
Ⓑ more bigger
Ⓒ more big
Ⓓ Correct as it is

38. Ⓕ most worse
Ⓖ worser
Ⓗ worst
Ⓙ Correct as it is

39. Ⓐ more bad
Ⓑ baddest
Ⓒ worse
Ⓓ Correct as it is

40. Ⓕ most terrible
Ⓖ more terrible
Ⓗ most terriblest
Ⓙ Correct as it is

Number correct 20 21 22 23 24 25 26 27 28 29 30 31 32 33 34 35 36 37 38 39 40
Percent correct 50 53 55 58 60 63 65 68 70 73 75 78 80 83 85 88 90 93 95 98 100

Copyright © Houghton Mifflin Company. All rights reserved.

Copyright © Houghton Mifflin Company. All rights reserved.

Name _____

Adjectives (continued from page 16)

Proofreading 27–34. Proofread the paragraphs below. Find seven mistakes in comparing with adjectives. Find one mistake in using *a* or *an*. Correct the mistakes.

Example: The octopus is ~~nervouser~~ than its relative, the squid.
(more nervous)

The octopus and the squid are both mollusks. The octopus
is the ~~most~~ interesting animal of the two. Its brain is larger
(more)
than the squid's. In fact, the octopus is one of the ~~intelligentest~~
(most intelligent)
animals in the world. Only mammals are ~~more smart~~.
(smarter)
~~A~~ octopus lives a shy, quiet life. It swims here and there to
(An)
find food, but it is ~~happyest~~ at home in its cave at the bottom
(happiest)
of the sea. Crabs are its favorite food.

Of the many kinds of octopus, the ~~bigest~~ measures almost
(biggest)
thirty-two feet across. It lives in the North Pacific Ocean. The
~~most~~ smallest kind is only two inches wide. It lives in the
Indian Ocean.

The octopus will not usually bite a human being. The
~~worse~~ octopus bite ever happened off the coast of Australia
(worst)
in 1967.

Name _____

Capitalization and Punctuation

Correct Sentences Correct these sentences and run-ons. Cross out letters and add capital letters where they are needed. Add end marks.

1. come to our tea party.
2. didn't you receive an invitation ?
3. my mother is wearing her violet blouse do you like it?
4. how beautiful the table looks!
5. don't touch the flowers they are very delicate.

Names of People and Pets Correct these sentences. Cross out letters and add capital letters where they are needed.

6. First, jane franklin arrived with her father.
7. Her cat, zizi, came along too.
8. The guest of honor, dr. w. d. may, arrived next.
9. Soon aunt doris introduced everyone.
10. At noon, mother announced lunch.

Names of Places and Things Correct these sentences. Cross out letters and add capital letters where they are needed.

11. French people celebrate bastille day on july 14.
12. The best month for a visit to paris is september.
13. A popular sight in the city is the eiffel tower.
14. The newburg french club returned from a trip last monday.
15. Members visited mont blanc, a mountain in france.

Copyright © Houghton Mifflin Company. All rights reserved.

Name _____

Capitalization and Punctuation *(continued from page 19)*

Abbreviations Write the abbreviations for the underlined words.

16. Doctor Kim Chan   **Dr.**
17. 1462 Fair Oaks Road, Cleveland, Ohio   **Rd., OH**
18. Post Office Box 56   **P.O.**
19. Mister William Bailey Junior   **Mr., Jr.**
20. Friday, August 8   **Fri., Aug.**

Commas in a Series Add commas where they are needed.

21. Oscar, Ann, and Lamar put on a play.
22. Lamar wrote, practiced, and acted.
23. Oscar got scenery, costumes, and a curtain.
24. The play was funny, interesting, and enjoyable.

More Uses for Commas Add commas where they are needed.

25. Do you feel better, Isabel, than you did yesterday?
26. Yes, I'm going back to school tomorrow.
27. Well, I'll look forward to seeing you.
28. Hannah, do you understand our homework assignment?
29. Yes, let me explain it to you.

Quotation Marks Add quotation marks to each sentence that needs them. Underline any sentence that does not need quotation marks.

30. "Look out for the car!" shouted Pilar.
31. "Thanks! exclaimed Vera as she jumped out of the way.
32. Pilar asked, "Didn't you see it?"
33. Vera answered that she was daydreaming.
34. "Will you be more careful now?" asked Pilar.
35. Vera promised that she would.

Copyright © Houghton Mifflin Company. All rights reserved.

Copyright © Houghton Mifflin Company. All rights reserved.

Name _____

Capitalization and Punctuation *(continued from page 20)*

Quotations Correct each quotation. Add punctuation marks and capital letters where they are needed.

36. "Where are my fiddlers three?"asked Old King Cole.

37. Little Miss Muffet exclaimed,"these curds taste awful./!"

38. "That candlestick is too tall,"said Jack.

39. The owl warned the pussycat,"don't fall overboard./!"

Titles Write each title correctly.

40. highlights _____ **Highlights**

41. child of fire _____ **Child of Fire**

42. the downtown news _____ **The Downtown News**

43. number the stars _____ **Number the Stars**

Proofreading 44–49. Proofread the paragraph below. Find two mistakes in capital letters and four missing or incorrect punctuation marks. Correct the mistakes.

Example: The play is in a book called Plays for Special Days.

Ms. Bradley said that we will put on a play to celebrate Martin Luther King day. She asked, "Who wants to try out for the main parts?"Well, almost all of us raised our hands. I tried out for dr. King. So did Jason, Matt, and Carlos. What a shock it was when I actually got the part,I'm nervous about forgetting my lines, but Mom said that she'll help me rehearse.

Grade **4**: Unit 5 Capitalization and Punctuation

Copyright © Houghton Mifflin Company. All rights reserved.

Name _____

Capitalization and Punctuation *(continued from page 21)*

Capitalization and Punctuation 50–55. Read the passage and look at the numbered, underlined parts. Choose the answer that shows the best way to write each underlined part. Fill in the circle beside that answer.

The author Charles Dickens was born in england on February 7, 1812.
                                              (50)

Unfortunately, his father often had serious money troubles. Charles had to leave

school and go to work soon he got a job with a Newspaper in london. In 1836,
                      (51)   (52)

Dickens married miss catherine hogarth. That same year, he wrote and published
                    (53)

the pickwick papers, his first book. It was brilliant. it was funny. It was popular.
    (54)   (55)

50. Ⓐ England on february
    Ⓑ England on February
    Ⓒ england on february
    Ⓓ Correct as it is

51. Ⓕ work. soon
    Ⓖ work. Soon
    Ⓗ work? Soon
    Ⓘ Correct as it is

52. Ⓐ Newspaper in London
    Ⓑ newspaper in london
    Ⓒ newspaper in London
    Ⓓ Correct as it is

53. Ⓕ miss Catherine Hogarth
    Ⓖ Miss Catherine Hogarth
    Ⓗ Miss catherine hogarth
    Ⓘ Correct as it is

54. Ⓐ The pickwick papers
    Ⓑ The Pickwick Papers
    Ⓒ The Pickwick Papers
    Ⓓ Correct as it is

55. Ⓕ It was brilliant it was funny and it was popular.
    Ⓖ It was brilliant funny and popular.
    Ⓗ It was brilliant, funny, and popular.
    Ⓘ Correct as it is

Number correct	28	29	30	31	32	33	34	35	36	37	38	39	40	41	42	43	44	45
Percent correct	51	53	55	56	58	60	62	64	65	67	69	71	73	75	76	78	80	82

Number correct	46	47	48	49	50	51	52	53	54	55
Percent correct	84	85	87	89	91	93	95	96	98	100

Grade **4**: Unit 5 Capitalization and Punctuation

Copyright © Houghton Mifflin Company. All rights reserved.

Name _____

Pronouns

What Is a Pronoun? Circle the pronoun that takes the place of the underlined word or words.

1. "Hal and (I) hiked up into the canyon," Kit said.

2. The sun warmed Hal and Kit, and (they) slowed down.

3. "Soon the sun was beating down on (us)," the boys explained.

Subject Pronouns Write the subject pronoun that could take the place of the underlined word or words.

4. Bev and I take long rides on our bikes. **We** _____

5. The bikes stay in good repair. **They** _____

6. Sometimes Dad joins us for a trip. **he** _____

Object Pronouns Write the object pronoun that could take the place of the underlined words.

7. I took a picture of Nate and Eileen. **them** _____

8. Nate bought a dinosaur book for his sister. **her** _____

9. Eileen liked the book very much. **it** _____

Using I and me Underline the correct word or words in ( ).

10. Langston, Pepe, and (I, me) planned a party for Al.

11. Pepe asked Langston and (I, me) for help with the decorations.

12. (He and I, I and he) found some blue balloons.

Possessive Pronouns Write the possessive pronoun that could take the place of the underlined word or words.

13. Meg's prism is made of glass. I saw **her** _____ prism yesterday.

14. The sun's rays shine on us. **Its** _____ rays keep us warm.

15. The twins' cameras are new. **Their** _____ cameras use a new kind of film.

Copyright © Houghton Mifflin Company. All rights reserved.

Name _____

Pronouns *(continued from page 23)*

Contractions with Pronouns Write a contraction to replace the underlined words in each sentence.

16. I am fond of my pet, Ducky. **I'm**

17. She is a mammal with a broad, flat, hairless snout. **She's**

18. She laid two eggs, and they will hatch in ten days. **they'll**

19. We are giving her young to Mr. Marcos at the zoo. **We're**

Pronouns and Homophones Underline the correct word in ( ).

20. Is that (your, you're) puppy?

21. (Your, You're) giving it too much dog food.

22. (Its, It's) such a pretty puppy.

23. (There, Their, They're) are pretty ones next door too.

24. (There, Their, They're) eyes are especially beautiful.

25. (There, Their, They're) very noisy, though.

Proofreading 26–30. Proofread these paragraphs. Find four incorrect pronouns. Find one pronoun that is in the wrong position in the sentence. Correct the mistakes.

Example: I and Bernice visited Philadelphia and had a great time their.
    Bernice and I   **there**

Bernice and I took an exciting trip on a train. Our old neighbor, Mrs. Lincoln,
met her and I at the train station. I had not seen Mrs. Lincoln for almost two years.
    me
Mrs. Lincoln gave me a big hug. She said, "Your so tall now, Connie, and
    You're
what long hair you have! How do you do those braids? Their great!"
    They're   **They're**

Mrs. Lincoln drove us to her home near the river and served us some
delicious cold chicken sandwiches. That night us slept in a big brass bed
    we
with fat white pillows and soft, fluffy blankets. Mrs. Lincoln sang a lullaby to
me and Bernice from the porch below our window.
Bernice and me

Copyright © Houghton Mifflin Company. All rights reserved.

Copyright © Houghton Mifflin Company. All rights reserved.

Name _____

Pronouns *(continued from page 24)*

Pronouns 31–35. Read the passage all the way through once. Then look at the underlined parts. Decide if they need to be changed or if they are fine as they are. Choose the best answer from the choices given. Fill in the circle beside that answer.

Last week, me and my sister
$\underline{\hspace{3cm}}$
(31)

were jumping rope outside. Two of

our neighbors were arguing.

"You're tree is dropping leaves
    (32)

onto my driveway," said Mr.

Benoit to Mr. Benoit. He stared
                          (33)

angrily at him.

The argument seemed silly to

my sister and I. We began to giggle,
$\underline{\hspace{3cm}}$
(34)

and the men's faces turned red.

They stopped their quarrel and
$\underline{\hspace{3cm}}$
(35)

made peace.

31. Ⓐ my sister and me
    Ⓑ I and my sister
    Ⓒ my sister and I
    Ⓓ (No change)

32. Ⓕ Your
    Ⓖ You
    Ⓗ Your'
    Ⓙ (No change)

33. Ⓐ The man
    Ⓑ Mr. Benoit
    Ⓒ His neighbor
    Ⓓ (No change)

34. Ⓕ my sister and me. We
    Ⓖ my sister and I. Us
    Ⓗ I and my sister. We
    Ⓙ (No change)

35. Ⓐ They're
    Ⓑ There
    Ⓒ They
    Ⓓ (No change)

Number correct	18	19	20	21	22	23	24	25	26	27	28	29	30	31	32	33	34	35
Percent correct	51	54	57	60	63	66	69	72	75	78	81	84	85	89	91	94	97	100

Grade 4: Unit 6   Pronouns

Copyright © Houghton Mifflin Company. All rights reserved.

Name _____

Adverbs and Prepositions

What Is an Adverb? Underline each adverb. Circle the verb it describes.

1. Finally, my sister and I (left) the house.
2. Koko and I (ran) fast.
3. I opened the big library door, and we (went) inside.
4. The science movie soon (began).
5. Everyone (sat) quietly.

Comparing with Adverbs Write the correct form of the adverb in ( ).

6. Gwen arrives ___later___ than Pedro. (late)
7. Her train runs ___more slowly___ than his. (slowly)
8. Of all the kids, he lives ___nearest___ to the school. (near)
9. Of all the class, Gwen talks ___most cheerfully___. (cheerfully)
10. She eats her snack ___faster___ than Pedro. (fast)

Using good and well Write good or well to complete each sentence correctly.

11. Steve makes ___good___ waffles.
12. He cooks ___well___.
13. He is also ___good___ at sports.
14. Steve does many things ___well___.

Negatives Underline the correct word to complete each sentence.

15. We don't have (no, any) milk for breakfast.
16. Dad didn't buy (any, none) yesterday.
17. Won't (anybody, nobody) go to the store?
18. The stores (are, aren't) never open this early.

Copyright © Houghton Mifflin Company. All rights reserved.

Name _____

Adverbs and Prepositions *(continued from page 27)*

What Is a Preposition? For each sentence, underline the prepositional phrase once and the preposition twice.

19. The birds flew across the sky.
20. A crow landed on the pine.
21. The robin has straw in its beak.
22. The parrot talked during the TV show.
23. Birdseed was scattered over the snow.

Proofreading 24–27. Proofread the paragraph below. Find two mistakes in comparing with adverbs, one mistake in using *good* or *well*, and one mistake in using negatives. Correct the mistakes.

more
Example: None of our birds lay ~~most~~ frequently than my hen Annabel.

Annabel lays an egg almost every day. She has two chicks,
more quickly
Maynard and Bit. Bit comes to my call ~~quicklier~~ than
loudest
Maynard. Of all the chicks we've ever had, Maynard cheeps
~~louder~~. I can hear him well when I bring the food. Annabel
well
usually keeps him quiet, though. Both chicks mind Annabel
any / don't have no . . .
~~good~~. They don't have ~~no~~ real feathers yet. Soft yellow down

still covers them.

Copyright © Houghton Mifflin Company. All rights reserved.

Copyright © Houghton Mifflin Company. All rights reserved.

Name _____

Adverbs and Prepositions *(continued from page 28)*

Adverbs 28–35. Read each paragraph below. Choose the line that shows the mistake. Fill in the circle beside that answer. If there is no mistake, fill in the circle beside the last answer.

28. Ⓐ On Field Day, two teams
    Ⓑ played tug of war. The red
    Ⓒ team pulled hardest.
    Ⓓ (No mistakes)

29. Ⓕ Martina cooks good.
    Ⓖ She helps her father make
    Ⓗ dinner on weekends.
    Ⓙ (No mistakes)

30. Ⓐ I never got none of the
    Ⓑ strawberries. Someone
    Ⓒ else ate them all.
    Ⓓ (No mistakes)

31. Ⓕ Otto felt shy at the party.
    Ⓖ He didn't know nobody.
    Ⓗ He wanted to leave.
    Ⓙ (No mistakes)

32. Ⓐ Kaia danced in the show.
    Ⓑ Of all the dancers, she
    Ⓒ leaped higher.
    Ⓓ (No mistakes)

33. Ⓕ Joe and Sam mopped the
    Ⓖ floor. Sam worked more
    Ⓗ carefullier than Joe did.
    Ⓙ (No mistakes)

34. Ⓐ I took three trains. The last
    Ⓑ one traveled most fastest
    Ⓒ and most smoothly.
    Ⓓ (No mistakes)

35. Ⓕ Jasmine's mother paints
    Ⓖ well. She hasn't ever
    Ⓗ taken an art lesson.
    Ⓙ (No mistakes)

Number correct	18	19	20	21	22	23	24	25	26	27	28	29	30	31	32	33	34	35
Percent correct	51	54	57	60	63	66	69	72	75	78	81	84	85	89	91	94	97	100

Grade 4: Unit 7   Adverbs and Prepositions

Copyright © Houghton Mifflin Company. All rights reserved.

Writing a Personal Narrative *(continued from page 31)*

Proofreading 5–10. Proofread this personal narrative to fix the six mistakes. Use proofreading marks to make your corrections. **Answers are shown.**

- Find two mistakes in verb tense.
- Find one missing end mark.
- Find a group of words that is not a sentence. Fix it by adding it to a complete sentence.
- Find two misspelled words with a short vowel sound before a consonant.

Proofreading Marks
¶ Indent
∧ Add
ə Delete
≡ Capital letter
/ Small letter

The Dentist Drill Blues

visited
Last week I ~~visit~~ the dentist for a checkup. I had a nasty

surprise. Dr. Love said I needed a filling!
next
When I went back to the dentist the ∧ week, I was really

scared. I was sure the experience would be painful. Dr. Love

put on some nice music. She told me to relax and breathe
drilled
deeply. Then she ~~drill~~ my tooth. She filled the hole. I hardly
felt
∧ ~~feel~~ any pain. Finally, she told me I could leave.

On my way out ∧ Dr. Love gave me a new toothbrush. She

said I had been brave. "It was nothing," I said, and I meant it!

Copyright © Houghton Mifflin Company. All rights reserved.

Writing a Personal Narrative

Revising 1–4. Revise the following personal narrative, using the directions in the box. Use the space above each line, on the sides, and below the narrative for your changes. **Sample answers are shown.**

- Take out one unimportant sentence.
- Add at least one detail to a sentence, telling how the umbrella looked.
- Change one sentence into dialogue.
- Write an ending that tells how the story worked out.

The Useful Umbrella

a bright pink plastic
The ugliest present I ever received was an umbrella with a

map of the world on it. I stuck it in the back of a closet and

never used it. ~~It rains a lot in Seattle, where I live.~~

One night I had to draw a map of Spain. I had left my

social studies book at school, and I couldn't find a map at
"Hey!" said my sister, "What about that ugly umbrella?"
home. ~~My sister reminded me about the umbrella.~~

When I found the umbrella, I was so relieved. I opened the
I drew my map and then put the umbrella back in its dark
dusty folds, and there was Spain, clearly outlined and labeled!
corner. That ugly present had been useful after all!

Copyright © Houghton Mifflin Company. All rights reserved.

Copyright © Houghton Mifflin Company. All rights reserved.

Name _____

Writing a Personal Narrative *(continued from page 33)*

Write Your Personal Narrative Write your personal narrative based on the prompt on page 33. If you need more space, continue writing on another sheet of paper.

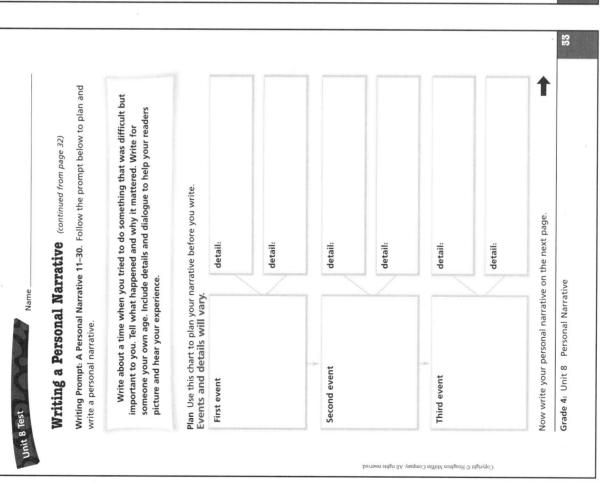

Remember to do these things to get a good score.

✔ Grab your readers' attention at the beginning.
✔ Use the pronoun *I*.
✔ Include only the important events, and tell them in order.
✔ Include details and dialogue that tell what you saw, heard, or felt.
✔ Write so that your narrative sounds like you.
✔ Tell how the experience worked out or how you felt at the end.
✔ Write complete sentences. Use what you have learned about capital letters, punctuation marks, and spelling. Use words correctly.

Personal narratives will vary.

Number correct	15	16	17	18	19	20	21	22	23	24	25	26	27	28	29	30
Percent correct	50	53	57	60	63	67	70	73	77	80	83	87	90	93	97	100

Grade 4: Unit 8   Personal Narrative

Copyright © Houghton Mifflin Company. All rights reserved.

Name _____

Writing a Personal Narrative *(continued from page 32)*

Writing Prompt: A Personal Narrative 11–30. Follow the prompt below to plan and write a personal narrative.

Write about a time when you tried to do something that was difficult but important to you. Tell what happened and why it mattered. Write for someone your own age. Include details and dialogue to help your readers picture and hear your experience.

Plan Use this chart to plan your narrative before you write. Events and details will vary.

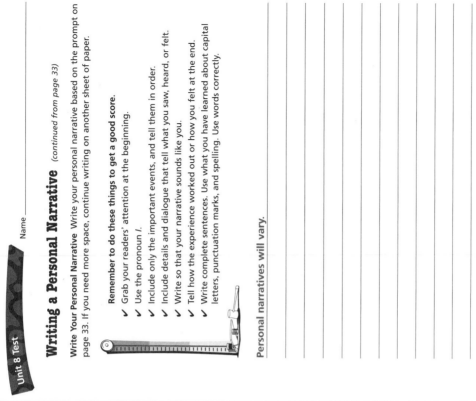

First event

detail:

detail:

Second event

detail:

detail:

Third event

detail:

detail:

Now write your personal narrative on the next page.

Grade 4: Unit 8   Personal Narrative

Name _____

Writing a Story

Revising 1–4. Revise the following paragraphs from a story, using the directions in the box. Use the space above each line, on the sides, and below the story for your changes. **Sample answers are shown.**

- Write a beginning sentence that introduces the problem.
- Add a sentence to the first paragraph to make the story sound sadder.
- Take out a sentence that is not important to the story.
- Add one example of dialogue to show what a character thinks or feels.

The Tail Tells the Tale

Cory stopped in front of an old cocker spaniel's cage. **Brownie was curled in a corner, quiet and still.** A sign said that his name was Brownie. Two rows away, playful puppies leaped and yelped. They would have no problem finding good homes.

"I want this old guy," said Cory. **"How will I know which dog to adopt?" wondered Cory as he and his mother entered the dog pound.**

~~Cory's mother said that she didn't agree.~~

Cory knelt in front of the old dog's cage and took a tennis ball out of his pocket. Sure enough, Brownie's eyes lit up! He dragged himself off the ground, and his tail began to wag.

Cory's mother smiled. ~~She was very tall.~~ "He's sort of cute after all," she said. "Let's take Brownie home."

"Do you really think we should adopt such a dull, old creature?" asked his mother.

Copyright © Houghton Mifflin Company. All rights reserved.

Name _____

Writing a Story *(continued from page 35)*

Proofreading 5–10. Proofread the following paragraphs from a story to fix the six mistakes. Use proofreading marks to make your corrections. **Answers are shown.**

- Find three mistakes in punctuating dialogue.
- Find one verb that doesn't agree with its subject.
- Find two misspelled words with the long *i* sound.

Proofreading Marks	
¶	Indent
∧	Add
~~	Delete
≡	Capital letter
/	Small letter

A Batty Lesson

"Did you remember to check the rabbit's water?" asked Dad.

Sarah shook her head. She stared at her book and tried to look busy.

"Please go out to the shed **right** now and check," said Dad.

"Take a flashlight," he added.

Sarah sighed. She hated going **outside** at night! Sarah went out back and ran across the lawn. Above her head, she heard scary flapping sounds. "Bats!" she shouted. She raced for the shed. Then Sarah sighed aloud, "You rabbits **drink** a lot of water, but I'll never forget to check it again!"

Copyright © Houghton Mifflin Company. All rights reserved.

Copyright © Houghton Mifflin Company. All rights reserved.

Name _____

Writing a Story *(continued from page 36)*

Writing Prompt: A Story 11–30. Follow the prompt below to plan and write a story.

Write a story for someone your age about a character who moves to a new house and finds a secret passageway. Who is the character? Where does the passageway lead? What happens when the character follows the passageway?

Plan Use this story map to plan your story before you write. **Characters, setting, and plot will vary.**

Characters	Setting	Plot
		Beginning:
		Middle:
		End:

Now write your story on the next page.

Copyright © Houghton Mifflin Company. All rights reserved.

Name _____

Writing a Story *(continued from page 37)*

Write Your Story Write your story based on the prompt on page 37. If you need more space, continue writing on another sheet of paper.

Remember to do these things to get a good score.

✔ Think of a plot with a beginning, a middle, and an end.
✔ Decide how your story will sound—scary? funny? serious? Choose details that help it sound this way.
✔ Introduce the main characters, the setting, and the problem in the beginning.
✔ In the middle, show how the characters deal with the problem. Tell only important events in an order that makes sense.
✔ Use details and dialogue to show rather than tell.
✔ In the end, tell how the problem works out.
✔ Write complete sentences. Use what you have learned about capital letters, punctuation marks, and spelling. Use words correctly.

Stories will vary.

Number correct	15	16	17	18	19	20	21	22	23	24	25	26	27	28	29	30
Percent correct	50	53	57	60	63	67	70	73	77	80	83	87	90	93	97	100

Name _____

Writing Instructions

Revising 1–4. Revise the following instructions, using the directions in the box. Use the space above each line, on the sides, and below the instructions for your changes. **Sample answers are shown.**

- Add the missing item to the sentence that lists the materials needed.
- Take out the sentence that does not belong.
- Add an order word.
- Move a step that is out of order.

Coaxing Flowers into Spring

It's easy to coax spring flowers to bloom early. All you
                    a bowl and
need are ˄some pebbles and a few bulbs. Narcissus bulbs work

                                                       Our ⌐
well. You can find everything you need at a garden center. ~~Our~~
~~garden center has cute lawn ornaments!~~
First,
˄ ⌐Fill the bowl about half full of pebbles. (Set the bowl in a

sunny spot once you have followed all the steps.)Then put the

bulbs on top of the pebbles, about one inch apart. Fill the rest

of the bowl with pebbles. Finally, add enough water to make

the bottom of each bulb wet. ⌐

After four to six weeks, beautiful flowers will appear.

You'll think spring has come early to your house!

Copyright © Houghton Mifflin Company. All rights reserved.

Name _____

Writing Instructions *(continued from page 39)*

Proofreading 5–10. Proofread this set of instructions to fix the six mistakes. Use proofreading marks to make your corrections. **Answers are shown.**

- Find two sentences that use two negatives together.
- Find two missing commas.
- Find two misspelled words with the long o sound.

Proofreading Marks	
¶	Indent
˄	Add
⌐	Delete
≡	Capital letter
/	Small letter

Make a Good Impression

How can you make great-looking cards,˄signs, and

invitations without spending a whole lot of money? Learn how

to rubber-stamp.

First, look in a craft store where stamping supplies are
sold
~~sould~~. ˄Find a rubber stamp that's right for your project. There

are hundreds to choose from! In addition, you will need a

colored ink pad,˄some markers, and paper. You don't need
any / don't   no ⌐
~~any / don't~~ ~~need no~~ . . .
           no ⌐
˄ ~~no~~special kind of paper. Just make sure it's not shiny, or the

ink won't stick.
                      coat
When you're ready, ~~cote~~˄the stamp with ink. Then press it
                                    ever / Don't / Never . . .
down hard on a piece of paper. Don't˄~~never~~ wiggle the stamp,

or the design will blur. Finally, use markers to write messages

around your design. The results are amazing! Everything you

make will look store-bought.

Copyright © Houghton Mifflin Company. All rights reserved.

Name _____

Writing Instructions *(continued from page 41)*

Write Your Instructions Write your instructions based on the prompt on page 41. If you need more space, continue writing on another sheet of paper. Sample instructions are shown.

Remember to do these things to get a good score.
✔ Begin with a topic sentence that tells what the instructions are about.
✔ Tell all the necessary materials.
✔ Include all the steps. Leave out anything that doesn't belong.
✔ Put the steps in the correct order. Use order words.
✔ Include exact details that make each step clear.
✔ Write a closing sentence that wraps up the instructions.
✔ Write complete sentences. Use what you have learned about capital letters, punctuation marks, and spelling. Use words correctly.

Have you ever heard the tinkling and jingling of wind chimes? You can make your own wind chime by following these simple instructions. You will need scissors, rope, a small clay flowerpot, string, a seashell, and a wire hanger.

First, cut a piece of rope about two feet long. Second, tie a large knot in one end of the rope. Now, thread the unknotted end of the rope through the hole in the bottom of the clay pot, from the inside out. Next, tie a piece of string around the seashell. Then tie the string to the rope knot inside the pot. Remember that the bottom edge of the shell should hang slightly beneath the bottom edge of the flowerpot. Finally, tie the rope to the hanger. Hang your wind chime in a special outdoor place and wait for the breezes to blow!

Number correct 15 16 17 18 19 20 21 22 23 24 25 26 27 28 29 30
Percent correct 50 53 57 60 63 67 70 73 77 80 83 87 90 93 97 100

Grade 4: Unit 10 Instructions

42

Copyright © Houghton Mifflin Company. All rights reserved.

Copyright © Houghton Mifflin Company. All rights reserved.

Name _____

Writing Instructions *(continued from page 40)*

Writing Prompt: Instructions 11–30. Follow the prompt below to plan and write a set of instructions.

These pictures show how to make a wind chime. Look carefully at each picture. Then write instructions to go along with the pictures. Write for someone your age.

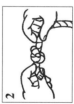

Plan Use this Step-by-Step Chart to plan your instructions before you write. Sample details are shown.

Steps	Materials Needed	Details
1. First, cut a piece of rope.	scissors	
2. Second, tie a large knot in the rope.	rope	
3. Now, thread the unknotted end of the rope through the clay pot.	clay flowerpot	
4. Next, tie string around the seashell.	string	thread from the inside out
5. Then tie the string to the rope knot.	seashell	
6. Finally, tie the rope to the hanger. Then hang your wind chime.	wire hanger	bottom edge of shell hanging beneath flowerpot

Now write your instructions on the next page.

Grade 4: Unit 10 Instructions

41

Name _____

Writing a Research Report

Revising 1–5. Revise the following paragraphs from a research report, using the directions in the box. Use the space above each line, on the sides, and below the report for your changes. **Sample answers are shown.**

- Rewrite the opening so that it is more interesting.
- Add a topic sentence to the beginning of the third paragraph.
- Take out two sentences that tell opinions rather than facts.
- Add a closing sentence that sums up the ideas in the report.

The Water Boatman

~~Here's my report. It's about an insect called a water boatman.~~ **What looks like a boat but acts like a tiger? It's a funny-looking insect called the water boatman!**

It is easy to see how the water boatman got its name. Its body is shaped like a long, thin canoe, and its strong back legs stick out like oars. The water boatman has two breathing holes on its abdomen. These holes stick out of the water and allow the insect to breathe while swimming on its back. ~~It's a pretty homely insect, if you ask me.~~

The water boatman eats many things. It gobbles up underwater insects. It also attacks and eats tadpoles and small fish. ~~I feel badly for the cute little tadpoles.~~ The water boatman grabs prey with its front legs. **The boatman might look silly, but if it's hungry, look out!** Then it kills the prey with poison from its mouth.

Copyright © Houghton Mifflin Company. All rights reserved.

43

Name _____

Writing a Research Report (continued from page 43)

Proofreading 6–10. Proofread these paragraphs from a research report to fix the five mistakes. Use proofreading marks to make your corrections. **Answers are shown.**

- Find two mistakes in capitalization.
- Find one place where a new paragraph should begin.
- Find two misspelled words with the final |ər| sound.

Proofreading Marks
¶ Indent
∧ Add
ᵔ Delete
≡ Capital letter
/ Small letter

An Actor's Life

In some ways, being an actor is like playing dress-up. In other ways, acting is much harder.

An actor has to make the story seem real. To do this, he or she must move and speak like someone else. A famous Russian acting **teacher** at the Onstage ≡academy says that actors even need to *feel* their characters' emotions! ¶Becoming an actor can take years of study. Acting students must learn how to run, walk, dance, sit, and fight on stage. They have to practice crying real tears and screaming with **terror.** Acting students will often try many different kinds of drama, from plays by ≡shakespeare to soap operas, before finding out which they do best.

Copyright © Houghton Mifflin Company. All rights reserved.

44

Copyright © Houghton Mifflin Company. All rights reserved.

Name _____

Writing a Research Report *(continued from page 44)*

Write a Paragraph for a Research Report 11–30. Write a paragraph for a research report about different forms of measurement, using the facts in the outline below. Sample paragraph is shown.

Remember to do these things to get a good score.

✓ Write a topic sentence that states the main idea.

✓ Use facts and details that support the main idea.

✓ Write complete sentences. Use what you have learned about capital letters, punctuation marks, and spelling. Use words correctly.

I. Early measurements
  A. A fathom—the distance between two outstretched arms—used to measure the depth of the sea
  B. A hand—the length of a human hand—used to measure the height of a horse
  C. A foot—a unit of distance—based on the length of a Roman soldier's foot
  D. A yard—a unit of distance—the length of England's King Henry I's arm

Early measurements were based on the parts of the body. A fathom was the distance between two arms outstretched. This measurement was used to measure the depth of the sea. The hand, which was used to measure the height of a horse, was based on the length of the human hand. A foot, a measure of distance, was based on the length of a Roman soldier's foot. A yard, a measure of length, was based on the length of a king's arm! This king was Henry I of England.

_____

_____

_____

Number correct 15 16 17 18 19 20 21 22 23 24 25 26 27 28 29 30
Percent correct 50 53 57 60 63 67 70 73 77 80 83 87 90 93 97 100

Grade 4: Unit 11 Research Report

Copyright © Houghton Mifflin Company. All rights reserved.

Page 47

Name _____

Writing to Express an Opinion

Revising 1-4. Revise the following paragraphs from an opinion essay, using the directions in the box. Use the space above each line, on the sides, and below the essay for your changes. Sample answers are shown.

- Rewrite the opening so that the topic of the essay is clear.
- Move one sentence that is out of place.
- Write a sentence to elaborate the final reason in the second paragraph.
- Write a topic sentence for the third paragraph.

Hot Season, Cool Camp

For fun and adventure, Red Hill Camp can't be beat. I look forward
to going back again every summer.
⋀ My town is interesting. There are lots of camps nearby.
Red Hill, Pine Knoll, Salt Meadow.

It's hard to say what I like most about Red Hill Camp. I really enjoy learning about nature. I love splashing through the muddy pond and finding lime green frogs! Then, after the rain, swarms of mosquitoes by the pond can ruin the canoeing. Another thing I like is that you make new friends. Last year, I ended up hanging around with different kids from those I hung out with at school. Finally, the food in the dining hall is delicious! ⋀ The chili is really tasty, and the pizza melts in your mouth.

There are a few things about Red Hill Camp that I don't enjoy. ⋀ On hot days, the three-mile hikes feel way too long. On rainy days, we can't play outside. Some mornings, when I hear my alarm ring at 7:00 A.M., I feel like just staying in bed.

Copyright © Houghton Mifflin Company. All rights reserved.

Page 48

Name _____

Writing to Express an Opinion *(continued from page 47)*

Proofreading 5-10. Proofread the following paragraphs from an opinion essay to fix the six mistakes. Use proofreading marks to make your corrections. Answers are shown.

- Find two places where a pronoun doesn't agree with the noun it replaces.
- Find two mistakes in forming contractions.
- Find two misspelled words with suffixes.

Proofreading Marks	
¶	Indent
⋀	Add
⌿	Delete
≡	Capital letter
／	Small letter

Highway Ups and Downs

Each year when our family drives four hundred miles to Chicago, my sister and I groan. We girls don't like going
don't
because long car trips bore us. Every hour seems endless! We
endless
can't read because we'll start to feel carsick. We get stiff and
we'll
uncomfortable. Also, we argue over the radio. Should they be
it
on an AM or an FM station? How high should the volume be?

These trips have their good points, however. We play word games and spot license plates. In addition, my parents pack great surprises, such as snacks and playing cards. You let us
They
bring along our favorite tapes too. Then there's the most wonderful part of all—arriving at our destination!
wonderful

Copyright © Houghton Mifflin Company. All rights reserved.

Copyright © Houghton Mifflin Company. All rights reserved.

Name _____

Writing to Express an Opinion (continued from page 49)

Write Your Opinion Essay Write your opinion essay based on the prompt on page 49. If you need more space, continue writing on another sheet of paper.

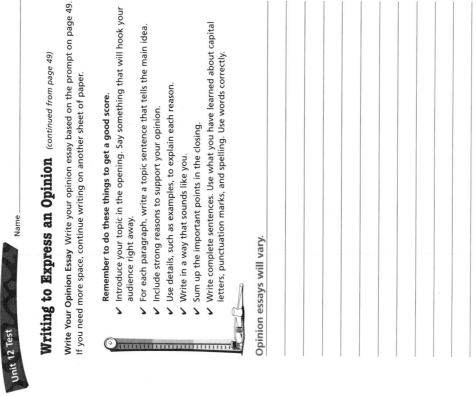

Remember to do these things to get a good score.

✔ Introduce your topic in the opening. Say something that will hook your audience right away.

✔ For each paragraph, write a topic sentence that tells the main idea.

✔ Include strong reasons to support your opinion.

✔ Use details, such as examples, to explain each reason.

✔ Write in a way that sounds like you.

✔ Sum up the important points in the closing.

✔ Write complete sentences. Use what you have learned about capital letters, punctuation marks, and spelling. Use words correctly.

Opinion essays will vary.

Number correct	15	16	17	18	19	20	21	22	23	24	25	26	27	28	29	30
Percent correct	50	53	57	60	63	67	70	73	77	80	83	87	90	93	97	100

Grade 4: Unit 12   Opinion

Copyright © Houghton Mifflin Company. All rights reserved.

Name _____

Writing to Express an Opinion (continued from page 48)

Writing Prompt: An Opinion Essay 11–30. Follow the prompt below to plan and write an opinion essay.

Write an opinion essay about the place where you live. **Tell someone who is your age what you like and don't like about living in that location.**

Plan Use the clusters below to plan your essay before you write. Use both clusters, one for the things you like and one for the things you don't like. **Opinions, reasons, and details will vary.**

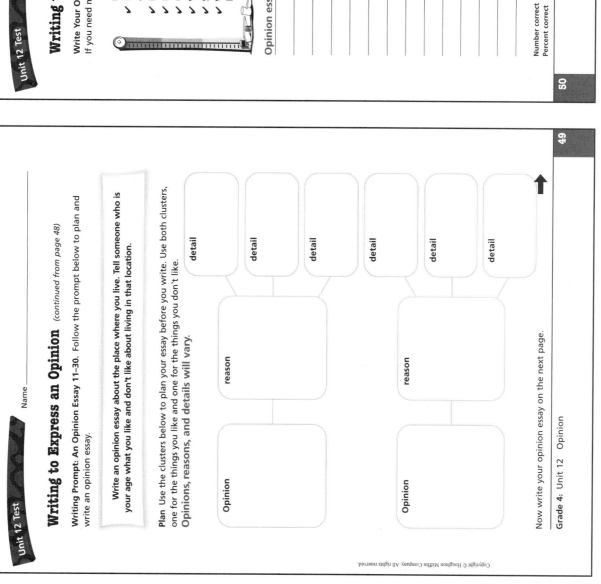

Now write your opinion essay on the next page.

Grade 4: Unit 12   Opinion

Writing to Persuade *(continued from page 51)*

Proofreading 5–10. Proofread the following paragraph from a persuasive essay to fix the six mistakes. Use proofreading marks to make your corrections. **Answers are shown.**

- Find two mistakes with making comparisons with adverbs.
- Find two mistakes in forming possessive nouns.
- Find two misspelled words with the |ôr| sound.

Proofreading Marks
¶ Indent
∧ Add
⌐ Delete
≡ Capital letter
/ Small letter

From Basement to Family Fun Center

Let's turn our dusty old basement into a family fun center!

With one central place for all of the kids' stuff, the rest of the house would stay cleaner. Jasons band could practice in the kitchen. I would study a lot **harder** ~~hardest~~ than I do now if I had a place to spread out and work. Of all three kids, little Tina plays the **loudest** ~~louder~~. If we had a fun center, she could ride her tricycle, gallop around on her toy horse, and roar like a lion without disturbing anybody. **For** peace and quiet in the rest of the house, we need a family fun center.

Grade 4: Unit 13   Persuasion

52

Copyright © Houghton Mifflin Company. All rights reserved.

Writing to Persuade

Revising 1–4. Revise the following paragraph from a persuasive essay, using the directions in the box. Use the space above each line, on the sides, and below the narrative for your changes. **Sample answers are shown.**

- Write an opening sentence that states the goal of the essay.
- Write a topic sentence for the second paragraph.
- Find the supporting sentence that tells an opinion. Rewrite it as a fact or an example.
- Write a closing sentence that sums up the goal and the reasons.

Say Yes to Uniforms!

Schools should have a policy that students wear uniforms.

First, school uniforms would be good for students. The uniform would remind students that they are at school to do a job. Students would fool around less and study more. If all students at school dressed the same, they would feel more like

There would be less pressure on students to dress in expensive, trendy clothes.

part of a group. It's dumb that only some lucky kids get to wear the expensive, trendy clothes.

Second, school uniforms would be a big help to families.

Parents would know just where to buy school clothes. They could save money by passing uniforms from child to child because the uniforms would always be in fashion. There would be fewer arguments between parents and children about what's

Schools uniforms make sense for everyone.

okay to wear to school.

Grade 4: Unit 13   Persuasion

51

Copyright © Houghton Mifflin Company. All rights reserved.

Copyright © Houghton Mifflin Company. All rights reserved.

Page 53

Name _____

Writing to Persuade *(continued from page 52)*

Writing Prompt: A Persuasive Essay 11–30. Follow the prompt below to plan and write a persuasive essay.

> Think about a club or an activity that you would like to join. Write an essay to persuade a parent or other adult to allow you to join.

Plan Use this web to plan your essay before you write. Goals, reasons, and examples will vary.

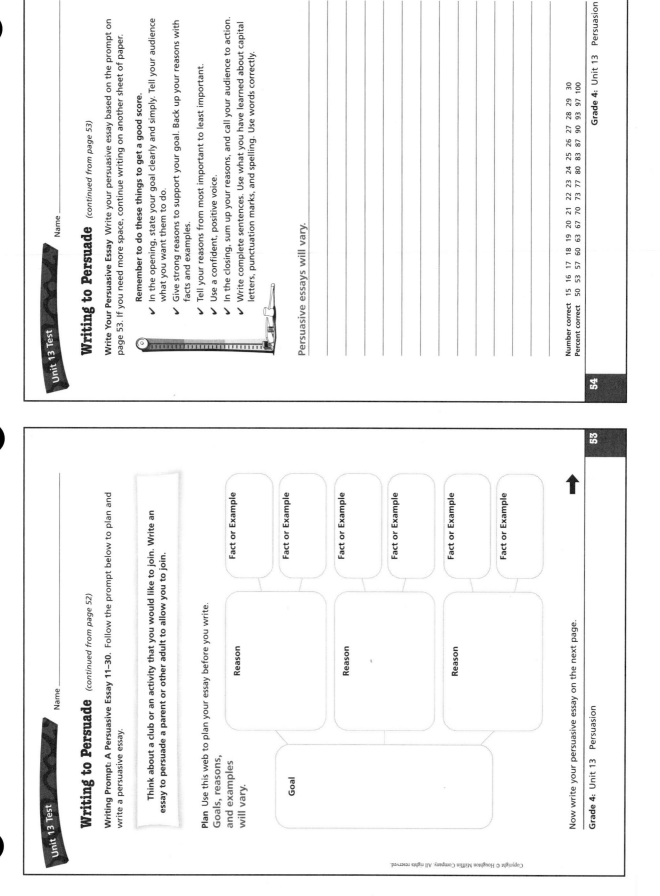

Now write your persuasive essay on the next page.

Copyright © Houghton Mifflin Company. All rights reserved.

53

Page 54

Name _____

Writing to Persuade *(continued from page 53)*

Write Your Persuasive Essay Write your persuasive essay based on the prompt on page 53. If you need more space, continue writing on another sheet of paper.

Remember to do these things to get a good score.

✓ In the opening, state your goal clearly and simply. Tell your audience what you want them to do.
✓ Give strong reasons to support your goal. Back up your reasons with facts and examples.
✓ Tell your reasons from most important to least important.
✓ Use a confident, positive voice.
✓ In the closing, sum up your reasons, and call your audience to action.
✓ Write complete sentences. Use what you have learned about capital letters, punctuation marks, and spelling. Use words correctly.

Persuasive essays will vary.

Number correct	15	16	17	18	19	20	21	22	23	24	25	26	27	28	29	30
Percent correct	50	53	57	60	63	67	70	73	77	80	83	87	90	93	97	100

Copyright © Houghton Mifflin Company. All rights reserved.

54

Unit 1: The Sentence

Sentences If a group of words below is a sentence, write it correctly. If it is not, write *not a sentence*.

1. the blizzard lasted all night
   The blizzard lasted all night./!

2. did you look outside in the morning
   Did you look outside in the morning?

3. was covered with snow
   not a sentence

Subjects and Predicates Draw a line between the complete subject and the complete predicate. Then underline each simple subject once and each simple predicate twice.

4. My younger brother | plays the violin.

5. His music teacher | gives lessons after school.

6. The students in the class | tune their instruments.

Run-on Sentences Rewrite each run-on sentence correctly. Sample answers are shown.

7. The dragon opened its jaws a flame shot out.
   The dragon opened its jaws. A flame shot out.

8. A princess came out of the castle, she turned on a hose.
   A princess came out of the castle. She turned on a hose.

9. The dragon ran away the princess grinned.
   The dragon ran away. The princess grinned.

Unit 2: Nouns

Kinds of Nouns Underline each noun. Then write each proper noun correctly.

10. His sister goes to a college in michigan. Michigan

11. The doctor gave aunt nancy some medicine. Aunt Nancy

12. Our town celebrates may day at emerson park. May Day, Emerson Park

Copyright © Houghton Mifflin Company. All rights reserved.

Unit 2: Nouns *(continued from page 55)*

Singular and Plural Nouns Write the plural of each noun.

13. kiss	kisses	16. discovery	discoveries
14. woman	women	17. peach	peaches
15. donkey	donkeys	18. tooth	teeth

Possessive Nouns Write each group of words another way. Use the possessive form of each underlined noun.

19. tail of a cat   a cat's tail

20. tools owned by carpenters   carpenters' tools

21. store for women   women's store

Unit 3: Verbs

Main and Helping Verbs Draw one line under the main verb and two lines under the helping verb.

22. They were trying their best.

23. Tanya had discovered the answer.

24. The summer was coming to an end.

25. Moths will eat holes in a sweater.

Present, Past, and Future Underline the verb in each sentence. Then write *present, past,* or *future.*

26. A loud car horn startled me.   past

27. That rubber barrel catches the rain.   present

28. I will practice my piano piece later tonight.   future

Agreement and Spelling the Present Tense Write the correct present-tense form of the verb in ( ). If it is correct as it is, write *correct.*

29. Gabriel (sing) with the chorus every Sunday.   sings

30. My rabbit's nose often (twitch) nervously.   twitches

31. We (remember) the way to your apartment building.   correct

32. That silver trailer (carry) two champion horses.   carries

Copyright © Houghton Mifflin Company. All rights reserved.

Copyright © Houghton Mifflin Company. All rights reserved.

Name _____

Unit 3: Verbs *(continued from page 56)*

Past Tense and the Past with Helping Verbs Underline the correct verb form in ( ).

33. My sister (taped, tapped) politely on my bedroom door.

34. The farmers (worried, worryed) about dry weather.

35. I (has, have) solved the problem at last!

36. Marissa has (threw, thrown) two strikes and a ball.

37. Our class (sang, sung) "America the Beautiful" at the assembly.

The Special Verb be Underline the correct form of the verb *be* in ( ).

38. I (is, am)

39. you (was, were)

40. people (was, were)

41. Jake (is, are)

42. winter (was, were)

43. they (is, are)

Contractions with *not* Write the contractions for the following words.

44. could not _____ couldn't

45. have not _____ haven't

46. will not _____ won't

47. does not _____ doesn't

Unit 4: Adjectives

Adjectives Underline each adjective. Circle the noun it describes. Do not underline *a*, *an*, and *the*.

48. I saw a strange (flower).

49. It had five huge (petals).

50. (They) were red and pink.

51. The (stem) was fuzzy.

Using *a*, *an*, and *the* Underline the correct article in ( ).

52. (a, an) airplane

53. (an, the) ice cubes

54. (a, an) number

Comparisons Write the correct form of the adjective in ( ).

55. Donelle was the (happy) girl in the class! _____ happiest

56. This slice of bacon is (thin) than that one. _____ thinner

57. The old chair is (comfortable) than the new one. _____ more comfortable

58. That was the (bad) vacation I have ever taken. _____ worst

59. The plum is (good) than the pear. _____ better

Copyright © Houghton Mifflin Company. All rights reserved.

Name _____

Unit 5: Capitalization and Punctuation

Correct Sentences Write these sentences correctly.

60. what gorgeous apples those are how many shall we get
What gorgeous apples those are! How many shall we get?

61. my brother is taking me to the movies would you like to come
My brother is taking me to the movies. Would you like to come?

62. do you like cheese pizza with onions help yourself to a slice
Do you like cheese pizza with onions? Help yourself to a slice.

Proper Nouns and Titles Find the proper nouns and the titles in these sentences. Write them correctly.

63. On monday, dr. emeka omaliko will arrive from nigeria.
Monday, Dr. Emeka Omaliko, Nigeria

64. I think bingo chewed up my favorite magazine, american girl.
Bingo, American Girl

65. What a great time I had with grandfather on new year's day!
Grandfather, New Year's Day

66. My aunt went to barton books and bought me a book called mystery in the mirror.
Barton Books, Mystery in the Mirror

Abbreviations Write an abbreviation for each word.

67. Junior _____ Jr.

68. Tuesday _____ Tues.

69. Doctor _____ Dr.

70. Avenue _____ Ave.

71. September _____ Sept.

72. January _____ Jan.

Commas Add commas where they are needed.

73. Gulls, swans, and ducks are all birds that can swim.

74. Did you see the weather report on TV, Charlotte?

75. Yes, it predicted rain and sleet.

76. The problem, Mom, is that I can't find my boots.

Unit 5: Capitalization and Punctuation (continued from page 58)

Quotations Rewrite the following sentences. Add punctuation marks and capital letters where they are needed. If a sentence is fine as it is, write *correct*.

77. where are you going with those pots and pans asked Amalia.
"Where are you going with those pots and pans?" asked Amalia.

78. Niko answered we're going to a parade for Groundhog Day.
Niko answered, "We're going to a parade for Groundhog Day."

79. Amalia asked what the pots and pans were for.
correct

80. everyone bangs on them to wake the groundhog replied Niko.
"Everyone bangs on them to wake the groundhog," replied Niko.

Unit 6: Pronouns

Subject, Object, and Possessive Pronouns Replace each underlined word or words with the correct pronoun.

81. John climbed into the canoe. ___**He**___
82. John pushed John's canoe away from the bank. ___**his**___
83. John waved to Mother and Father. ___**them**___
84. His mother called to John, "Be careful!" ___**him**___
85. The parents got into the parents' car and drove off. ___**their**___

I and me and **Homophones** Underline the word or words that complete each sentence correctly.

86. (Your, You're) a good in-line skater.
87. Mrs. Brown thanked (James and I, James and me) for helping her.
88. (Ellie and me, Ellie and I) take the same bus to school.
89. All of the students put (their, there) backpacks in the closet.
90. Will you play basketball with (me and Sean, Sean and me)?
91. A raccoon stuck (it's, its) nose into the garbage can.

Copyright © Houghton Mifflin Company. All rights reserved.

Unit 6: Pronouns (continued from page 59)

Contractions with Pronouns Write the contraction for each of the following words.

92. we are ___**we're**___   94. you will ___**you'll**___
93. I have ___**I've**___   95. I am ___**I'm**___

Unit 7: Adverbs and Prepositions

What Is an Adverb? Underline each adverb. Circle the verb it describes.

96. Tyler (sang) the song sweetly.
97. I finally (found) my favorite cap.
98. A scared kitten (ran) inside.
99. Now I (understand) this math problem.

Comparing with Adverbs Write the correct form of the adverb in ( ).

100. Can you see the star that shines (clearly) of all? ___**most clearly**___
101. Juno writes (fast) than I do. ___**faster**___
102. Of all the dogs, the spaniel jumped (high). ___**highest**___
103. Charles behaves (politely) than his brother. ___**more politely**___

Using *good* and *well* and Negatives Underline the correct word to complete each sentence.

104. I haven't (ever, never) skied.
106. We don't have (any, no) paper.
105. Stir the soup (good, well).
107. She learned her lesson (good, well).

What Is a Preposition? Draw one line under each prepositional phrase and two lines under each preposition.

108. The ball dropped through the basket.
109. Roberto was resting on a park bench.
110. I can hardly wait until Saturday.

Number correct	55	56	57	58	59	60	61	62	63	64	65	66	67	68	69	70	71	72	73	74
Percent correct	50	51	52	53	54	55	56	57	58	59	60	61	62	63	64	65	66	67		

Number correct	75	76	77	78	79	80	81	82	83	84	85	86	87	88	89	90	91	92	93	94
Percent correct	68	69	70	71	72	73	74	75	76	77	78	79	80	81	82	83	84	85		

Number correct	95	96	97	98	99	100	101	102	103	104	105	106	107	108	109	110
Percent correct	86	87	88	89	90	91	92	93	94	95	96	97	98	99	100	

Copyright © Houghton Mifflin Company. All rights reserved.

Individual Record Form

UNIT	POSSIBLE SCORE	NUMBER CORRECT	PERCENT CORRECT
Getting Started: Writing a Description	20		
1 The Sentence	40		
2 Nouns	45		
3 Verbs	60		
4 Adjectives	40		
5 Capitalization and Punctuation	55		
6 Pronouns	35		
7 Adverbs and Prepositions	35		
8 Writing a Personal Narrative	30		
9 Writing a Story	30		
10 Writing Instructions	30		
11 Writing a Research Report	30		
12 Writing to Express an Opinion	30		
13 Writing to Persuade	30		
End-of-Year Grammar Test	110		

Copyright © Houghton Mifflin Company. All rights reserved.

Class Record Form

Name	UNITS														
	Getting Started: Writing a Description	1 The Sentence	2 Nouns	3 Verbs	4 Adjectives	5 Capitalization and Punctuation	6 Pronouns	7 Adverbs and Prepositions	8 Writing a Personal Narrative	9 Writing a Story	10 Writing Instructions	11 Writing a Research Report	12 Writing to Express an Opinion	13 Writing to Persuade	End-of-Year Grammar Test
1.															
2.															
3.															
4.															
5.															
6.															
7.															
8.															
9.															
10.															
11.															
12.															
13.															
14.															
15.															
16.															
17.															
18.															
19.															
20.															
21.															
22.															
23.															
24.															
25.															
26.															
27.															
28.															
29.															
30.															
31.															
32.															
33.															
34.															
35.															

Copyright © Houghton Mifflin Company. All rights reserved.